Understanding Disability

From Theory to Practice

Second Edition

MICHAEL OLIVER

First edition 1996
Reprinted twelve times
Second edition 2009

Published by
PALGRAVE MACMILLAN

Palgrave Macmillan in the UK is an imprint of Macmillan Publishers Limited, registered in England, company number 785998, of Houndmills, Basingstoke, Hampshire RG21 6XS.

Palgrave Macmillan in the US is a division of St Martin's Press LLC, 175 Fifth Avenue, New York, NY 10010.

Palgrave Macmillan is the global academic imprint of the above companies and has companies and representatives throughout the world.

Palgrave® and Macmillan® are registered trademarks in the United States, the United Kingdom, Europe and other countries.

ISBN 978–0–230–22028–7

This book is printed on paper suitable for recycling and made from fully managed and sustained forest sources. Logging, pulping and manufacturing processes are expected to conform to the environmental regulations of the country of origin.

A catalogue record for this book is available from the British Library.

A catalog record for this book is available from the Library of Congress.

10 9 8 7 6 5 4 3
18 17 16 15 14 13 12 11

Printed and bound in China

To John the bladder man and catheter queen Jane
for the peace of mind I needed to complete this project.
To Alice, Georgina and Charley
just because I love them.

Contents

List of Figures and Tables

Figures

Table

Acknowledgements

There are three people without whom this book could not have been completed.

My wife Joy not only for her love and companionship but also for her secretarial skills, which gave order to the chaos I created in preparing the manuscript, and for saving my laptop from disappearing out of the window on more than one occasion.

My friends and colleagues Len Barton and Colin Barnes have influenced not just my work but my life as well. They are great to bounce ideas off and even better to hang out with, especially if alcohol and music are involved.

MICHAEL OLIVER

The authors and publishers wish to thank the following for permission to use copyright material: Sony/ATV Music Publishing (UK) Ltd for permission to reproduce the lyrics of Leonard Cohen and Bob Dylan. All rights reserved; Lois Keith for the poem 'Tomorrow I'm Going to Re-write the English Language' from L. Keith (ed.) *Mustn't Grumble*, London: The Women's Press (1994); Disability Press, for material reproduced in Chapter 3 originally by M. Oliver in C. Barnes and G. Mercer (eds) *Implementing the Social Model of Disability: Theory and Research*, Leeds: Disability Press (2004); McGraw-Hill Education, for material in Chapter 4 originally by M. Oliver in K. Rosenblum and T. Travis (eds) *The Meaning of Difference*, 3rd edn. New York: McGraw-Hill (2003); University of Ottawa Press, for material reproduced in Chapter 8 originally by M. Oliver in R. Flynn and R. Lemay (eds) *A Quarter Century of Normalization and Social Role Valorization Evolution and Impact*, Ottawa: University of Ottawa Press (1999); and Ann Macfarlane for the poem 'Watershed' from L. Keith (ed.) *Mustn't Grumble*, London: The Women's Press (1994). Coalition, for material in Chapter 9 originally from C. Barnes and M. Oliver, 'Disability Politics and the Disability Movement in Britain: Where Did It All Go Wrong?', *Coalition* (Aug 2006). Every effort has been made to trace all the copyright-holders, but if any have been inadvertently overlooked the publishers will be pleased to make the necessary arrangement at the first opportunity.

Notes on Contributors

Colin Barnes is Professor of Disability Studies and was the founding director of the Centre for Disability Studies at the University of Leeds.

Vic Finkelstein has been active in disability politics, trained as a clinical psychologist and was a senior lecturer at the Open University. He is now retired.

Beth Omansky is a community activist and disability studies scholar living in Portland, Oregon, USA.

Section 1

Experiencing and Challenging a Disabling World

Introduction

Please forgive me if I waste your time

Leonard Cohen was recently asked to write a preface to his novel *Beautiful Losers*, which was being translated into Chinese. He ended this preface with the following plea to his Chinese readership: 'Please forgive me if I have wasted your time.' When the publisher asked me to consider a second edition of *Understanding Disability* I had a similar reaction. After all, I had retired five years ago and, with one or two exceptions, had not read a book or written anything significant about disability. I was determined not to become a 'ghost' professor haunting my old colleagues and adversaries from somewhere beyond my ivory tower, secure in the knowledge that my emeritus status and ageing profile would keep me safe from the worst excesses of academic debate and vitriolic criticism. So my initial reaction was that such a venture would be a waste of your time and mine.

However, Catherine Gray at Palgrave Macmillan was both patient and persuasive and convinced me that I should think about what a second edition would look like, assuring me that, as the first edition had done very well and was still popular, there would be a market for a new version. The more I thought about this, the more attractive the idea became. While my first five years as a pensioner had been reasonably contented ones, I had not (yet) discovered the perfect horse-racing system to keep me in luxury during my dotage nor had my recent obsession with on-line poker given me untold riches. In fact, one of the lessons I have learned in the last five years is that it is a lot easier to bamboozle in academia than it is to bluff at the poker table. Were it not so I would be writing this in Barbados, which I can assure you I am not. Nor am I likely to get rich on the proceeds from this book, but, as the Tesco's advertisement says, 'every little helps'.

It would also be vain of me not to admit that I was flattered that people would still be willing to pay good money to read my words. I can't do the humility of Cohen in his preface to his Chinese readers because I do realize that I have made a substantial contribution to our

3

understanding of disability issues but I retired five years ago. I was also aware that many of the debates I had previously been involved in, and in some cases initiated, were still ongoing. The more I thought about it, the more attractive the opportunity to have a further say became. It was clear that I did not have the drive, desire or capacity to produce a book full of new material and, what's more, I no longer had the resources. After all, within two years of retirement I had given away all my books and, apart from seeing a couple of students get their PhDs and the odd social occasion, my links to the university had been virtually severed.

I was still not convinced that a second edition was a viable project so I took soundings from senior figures in disability studies. You see how quickly academic bull returns because what I actually did was ask Colin Barnes and Len Barton what they thought. All three of us had remained firm friends and occasional drinking companions since my retirement and I knew I could rely on them to tell me what they thought. They convinced me that the project was viable and that there was plenty of my material that could be incorporated into the new edition. I was becoming more attracted to the idea but my final concern was that I no longer had secretarial support and that I might never get the final manuscript together in one coherent whole. My wife Joy, who had recently given up her counselling and psychotherapy practice to join me in contented retirement, had been a secretary in a previous incarnation and offered her support. Even if her offer of help was really a ploy to drag me away from the Racing Channel or VCPoker.com, I had now run out of reasons not to go ahead.

The next stage was to put together a coherent proposal and, while I was anxious to retain the structure and ethos of the first edition, my initial thoughts were to only include material that had not been published elsewhere or not necessarily in easily accessible places. With the help of Catherine and two anonymous reviewers, it soon became clear that it would be sensible to include some material from the first edition and also to produce something new to take account of the issues and debates that have taken place since my retirement. I was concerned about the latter and made it clear that I was not going to embark on a crash course in disability studies to catch up with everything that has gone on since my retirement; I was assured that this was not necessary.

So what follows will be a mixture of some material from the first edition, some chapters and papers that have been published and presented elsewhere and some new material. It will not be an introduction to disability studies nor will it be an up-to-date resource designed to capture the essence of disability studies today. Rather it will be a link to my past writings, a collection of pre-retirement thoughts and insights and some post-retirement jottings liberally sprinkled with a few games I like to play and my own attempts at humour. It should be seen more as a journey than a description of my destination and, because of this, there may well be inconsistencies in the use of language and terminology, which have changed as my journey has progressed. In the rest of this introduction I will try to provide you with a map for that journey. I hope that you will not get lost along the way but please feel free to take as many detours as you wish and even the occasional break because all of the chapters can be read as stand-alone pieces.

Heading for the highlands

In reflecting on my own work I have been concerned with a number of different areas; notably theory, policy, practice and politics. Further, I have always believed that they are all inextricably linked; theory is not just designed to produce knowledge but to facilitate the development of policy; policy should be relevant to professional practice and helping people improve their lives; and that practice should take account of the political context in which it takes place and be allied to those groups working to produce social change. So in my work I have attempted to outline what a social theory of disablement would look like; to make a contribution to the development of social policy in respect of disabled people; to assist a variety of professionals in their interventions in the lives of disabled people; and to involve myself in a disability politics geared to eradicating the disabling barriers that disabled people face.

It would be wholly inappropriate for me to try to make any kind of judgement about how successful or otherwise I have been, as well as it being beyond the scope of this book. Instead, I want to use these areas as a way of explaining and perhaps justifying the choice of material that I have included in this book. In order to do this I decided to divide the contents into two sections. The first section is called 'Experiencing and Challenging a Disabling World' because the chapters contained therein reflect the way my own personal experiences of disablement grew into a broader understanding of the fact that we continue to live in a disabling world. The second section is called 'Theorizing and Changing a Disabling World' because the chapters are an attempt to produce socially useful knowledge which will play a part in challenging and hopefully changing this world.

Before explaining this further, it is necessary that I briefly outline the nature and contents of each chapter, as follows.

Section 1: Experiencing and Challenging a Disabling World

Chapter 1: From Personal Struggle to Political Understanding and Back Again
This will update the original Chapter 1 by discussing changes in both personal experiences and theoretical understandings that have occurred since the first edition was published in 1996. The updating will consist of a new final section.

Chapter 2: Mobility Impairment in a Social Context
This chapter was originally given as my professorial lecture and published in the first edition. It focuses on walking and how society responds to people who find this task difficult or impossible. It is based upon my own experiences of not walking and my own understanding of why society responds in particular ways.

Chapter 3: The Social Model: History, Critique and Response
The social model emerged from my encounter with a document called the *Fundamental Principles of Disability* (UPIAS, 1976), and the way it forced me to rethink my own experiences of impairment and disability. My formulation of it for my social work students became the key area of debate in disability studies for more than twenty years and was a central focus for the emerging disabled people's movement. This chapter will contain edited sections from Chapters 2 and 3 of the first edition of this book plus some new material.

Chapter 4: Unmet Promises of Disability Law and Policy
This chapter explores my own and a blind colleague's experiences of using public transport systems and their failures to take account of our needs. It then analyzes the implications for law and policy and suggests that transport systems have a long way to go before they adequately meet the needs of disabled travellers. It was co-written with an American colleague, Beth Omansky.

Chapter 5: Special Education into the Twenty-first Century
In this chapter I build upon some of my own personal experiences when I worked as a special education lecturer and attempt to show their implications not just for the development of special needs education

but education in general. It was originally given as a keynote address at the International Special Education Conference, 'Including the Excluded', Manchester, in 2000.

Section 2: Theorizing and Changing a Disabling World

Chapter 6: Disability and Normalization: A Critique

In 1994 I was invited to address a conference to celebrate twenty-five years of normalization and its achievements. I was specially invited to provide a critique of it and offer an alternative perspective. This I did and argued that materialist social theory offered disabled people a much more relevant and useful theory than normalization ever could. It was originally published in R. Flynn and R. Lemay (eds) (1999), *A Quarter Century of Normalization and Social Role Valorization: Evolution and Impact* (Ottawa: University of Ottawa Press).

Chapter 7: The Relevance of Emancipatory Research for Policy Development

Over the last fifteen years I have written a number of papers on methodology and have been in the forefront of advocating an emancipatory approach to disability research. This chapter brings together much of this work, as well as providing a critique of the recently revised World Health Organization (WHO) classification scheme. It was originally given at a conference in Dublin in 2002 organized by the Irish National Disability Authority.

Chapter 8: Disabling or Enabling Welfare: What Next for Disabled People?

No book about disability should ignore the possible disabling consequences of welfare provision nor its enabling potential. Therefore I have included a chapter on the topic, the original version of which was written by Colin Barnes and myself as the final chapter in a book on disability and social policy which we wrote in the late 1990s (Barnes and Oliver, 1998).

Chapter 9: Disability Politics and the Disabled People's Movement in Britain

The central concern of this chapter will be disability politics; it will suggest that the movement has failed to consolidate its early successes and will examine some of the main reasons for this. It will be suggested that disability politics has taken too narrow an approach to social change by concentrating too exclusively on disability rights. The original version of this was co-written with Colin Barnes and first appeared in the journal *Coalition* (Barnes and Oliver, 2006). The second half of the chapter is a response to our piece, written by Vic Finkelstein.

Chapter 10: Disablement into the Twenty-first Century
This is based upon the millennium lecture I gave at the University of Glasgow. As well as considering where we've been and where we're going as disabled people, it is in homage to Bob Dylan, the great American singer, songwriter and cultural icon, because his work has been a constant companion as I have struggled to understand myself and my place in the world.

Chapter 11: Personalizing the Political and Politicizing the Personal
This final chapter returns to the themes I tried to explore in the final chapter of the first edition; notably the relationship between the individual and the collective. It does this in the light of changing circumstances since the original publication, notably in disability politics, the disabled people's movement and disability studies. It is completely new and written specifically for this book.

Some direction home

As a sociologist, developing a social theory of disablement that incorporates both impairment and disability has always been very important for me. My book *The Politics of Disablement* (1990) was an initial attempt to sketch out what such a theory might look like but was never intended to be a final statement on the matter. Indeed, at the time of writing it in the 1980s it was impossible to undertake such a project for the necessary material was very thin on the ground. Since then there has been a great deal of work on the history, anthropology, psychology and politics of both disability and impairment but, in my view at least, this hasn't led to any further significant developments in generating a social theory of disablement.

There have been some attempts to bring impairment and disability into a more symbiotic relationship, sometimes by critics of my work who wrongly claim that I ignore impairment. There is not the space to deal with this again here, as really it is time to stop 'talking the talk' and start 'walking the walk'. Chapter 3 of this new edition does deal with mobility impairment and *The Politics of Disablement* contains a central chapter on it, and much of my empirical research has been concerned to give people the opportunity to talk about how they manage their impairments in a disabling world. Those who claim otherwise either haven't read my work or are promoting different agendas of their own or even themselves.

Functionalist social theory has also failed to offer any significant theoretical insights. The once fashionable sociology of deviance appears to have disappeared as the more marketable criminology takes over. Functionalist theory did underpin the rise of normalization, which rebranded itself as social role valorization to overcome its unfortunate connections to the idea of normality and the dangers of appearing to advocate that its main aim was 'to make people normal'. Chapter 6 is a critique of this whole approach, which now seems to have disappeared from our theoretical, policy and political agendas, although, as I understand it, many of its initial devotees now find themselves in the higher echelons of academia, policy development and service delivery.

More recently, a variety of post-structuralist and postmodernist theories have been advocated as the way forward for disablement theory. Apart from the fact that few people could understand them and their relevance, they have failed to provide any socially useful knowledge or insights that could be used in improving policy or service development for disabled people and their emancipatory potential remains shrouded in the mists of their own verbiage. Chapter 5 tries to expose some of these weaknesses in respect of education policy in general and special needs in particular. The latest incarnation, something called critical realism, also seems to be having problems explaining what realism 'really' means.

My own concern has always been to develop theory that is policy-relevant. In particular, I have been concerned to promote policies that will address and tackle the institutionalized discrimination that is faced in the disabling society. The research project that I directed for the British Council of Organizations of Disabled People (BCODP), which resulted in the publication of *Disabled People in Britain and Discrimination* by Colin Barnes (1991), was instrumental in forcing the British government to change its mind about anti-discrimination legislation. They could no longer deny that discrimination against disabled people was endemic to Britain because their own statistics proved it to be so. The fact that many who had fought so hard for the subsequent legislation found it a bitter disappointment is addressed more fully in Chapter 8.

This concern with policy was not solely confined to promoting measures to combat discrimination and, with Colin Barnes (1998), a general text on social policy was published. Policy issues are addressed throughout this book as well: Chapter 4 considers the lack of impact that anti-discrimination legislation has had on transport policy, both here and in the USA; Chapter 5 looks at education policy and Chapter 6 critically examines normalization's claim to be responsible for closing down many long-stay institutions; Chapter 7 considers the need for policy-relevant research, an issue to which I will return in the final two chapters.

Professional practice has been a central concern for most of my life. As a child the first professionals we encounter are usually our school teachers. Precisely how much of my grammar school failure was due to me being a stroppy teenager and how much to bad teaching is still something I cannot be sure about. When I was discharged from hospital after breaking my neck the community professionals I encountered weren't necessarily bad practitioners; they simply had nothing to offer me beyond their stereotypical attitudes which attempted to sell me the idea that I had been the victim of an appalling tragedy and that society had very little to offer me. My rejection of this view is explained in Chapters 1 and 2.

I can't claim to have consciously decided that, as a result of these unfortunate encounters, I was going to spend much of my professional life working to try to improve professional practice, but in reality I have. Over the years I have taught social workers, teachers, occupational therapists, doctors, nurses and researchers in a variety of different settings and too many courses to mention here. The main vehicle for this has been the social model of disability, which I named but did not invent in 1982. In other words, I may have been the godfather at the christening but I certainly wasn't the real father at the conception. The social model was originally developed to help social workers on a postgraduate course to think about their practice in new and different ways. Again, Chapter 2 will deal with this in more detail.

In the next chapter I describe my growing political awareness and some of the many influences upon me. But this growing political awareness is linked to the social model in an unexpected way. When I formulated it as a possible aid to social work practice I had no idea that it would also crucially become the slogan for the newly emerging disabled people's movement. Somebody once said (or if they didn't, they should have) all successful social movements either have a good slogan or a good song; hence CND had 'Ban The Bomb' and the Civil Rights movement had 'We Shall Overcome'. The disabled people's movement had 'The Social Model Of Disability'. Subsequent research that Jane Campbell and I (Campbell and Oliver, 1996) did on the history of the movement revealed the significant role the social model played in raising disabled people's consciousness of the need to create a collective social movement of our own.

While this was undoubtedly a good thing for the development of the movement, it has now become a sacred cow that has been viciously fought over during the last twenty years. What began its life as an aid to professional practice has been slaughtered on the altar of theory for not explaining everything about impairment and disability and has been defended in the training courses and journals of the chosen ones to the point that both sides have tried to make it into something it is not. Chapter 3 really is my final word on the subject, so, please, no more books or PhD theses about it, no more arguments in the classrooms of consciousness raising and no more fights on the streets of activism. If it is any good, use it and share your gains with the rest of us; if it is useless don't tell us so any more but invent something else.

Of course, disability politics and the drive for social change are not just about the social model. My initial, direct involvement in disability politics is discussed in the next chapter and, as well as writing two books on the subject, I have been involved as an activist on the streets and in several positions of responsibility within the disabled people's movement. My retirement five years ago was not just a retirement from the academy but from disability activism as well. I have continued to observe from afar, however, mainly to keep abreast of new developments in order to preserve my own hard-fought services in a society that promises me, and indeed all other disabled people, much but that delivers little except cuts in or threats to cut services. Chapter 8 will discuss the reasons why the political voice of disabled people is now much more muted despite this appalling situation and Chapter 9 will consider what is likely to happen in the future.

An underlying theme for all this is my own personal experience of both impairment and the disabling society and this underpins all the chapters. In the next chapter I try to make this explicit in a general way, and Chapters 3, 4 and 5 show how my own experiences of not walking, of transport systems and of education directly shaped my later thinking on the subjects. However, I would not want to suggest that I am any clearer now than I have ever been about the precise role of my personal experiences in shaping my academic work or that I will be able to be more definitive about this at the end of the book.

Bringing it home

In trying to make sense of it all I am reminded of a metaphor Robert Edgerton once used when asked to justify his research with people who the Americans used to call people with mental retardation. He characterized the world as one of darkness and that research was like a streetlight shining out into this darkness. For many years I saw my own work like that – trying to illuminate the darkness – but gradually I came to realize that there was a problem with this metaphor. While the more work I did the more the darkness was illuminated but this didn't seem to reduce the darkness. In fact, just the opposite was occurring – the more work I did the more I came to realize that, if anything, the darkness was growing, not reducing.

It is a sobering thought to realize that, while my work may have illuminated some of the darkness of the disabling society, for me at least it has hightlighted how much we don't know rather than how much we do. I hope that my reflections on my journey in the rest of this book will, therefore, at the very least help others to illuminate this darkness further; but, if they don't, I apologize in advance for wasting your time. If this turns out to be the case don't be too hard on me – great artists and scientists throughout history have grappled to illuminate this darkness between what we know and what we don't.

1

From Personal Struggle to Political Understanding and Back Again

Introduction

This first chapter originally appeared in the first edition of this book. I decided to include it again because it will still help to throw some light on why I have written the things that appear later in the book as it remains rooted in my own personal biography, which I briefly outline. In the earlier edition I threatened that a more detailed description of my life might one day appear as an autobiography or as a thinly disguised novel. I hope, at this later stage, that I can reassure anyone who might feel worried about featuring in either of those two enterprises that neither is now likely to appear. Having written more than a million words during my academic career I do not intend to spend my retirement slaving over a word processor and I cannot imagine that there is much of a readership out there wanting to hear more from me. So this may be your last opportunity.

This personal account will focus on four areas which, for analytical purposes, I will separate into (1) looking at my growing political awareness, (2) the way my career developed and the influence this had on my growing political consciousness, (3) my growing involvement with disabled people and the organizations which we were creating and the effect that this had on my developing understanding of disability as a personal, social and sociological phenomenon and (4) my gradual retreat from academic and political life in order to concentrate on other things, mainly doing nothing. Bobbie McGee knew the importance of this when she sang 'Nothing ain't worth nothing but it's free'.

The personal is the personal

My own personal experience of disability began in 1962. I was the only son of working-class parents and had recently left the local grammar school as a failure, having only gained three O levels. Stuck in a dead-end clerical job, my life centred around the cricket and football I played for local teams and the macho activities I and my mates often used to pretend to get up to, and occasionally actually did. When I was seventeen, five of us decided to go on holiday together, to a well-known holiday camp in Essex (the present-day equivalent of the package tour to Spain or Greece).

Behaving like latter-day lager louts, it was not long before I got up to something that was to transform my life. I dived into the holiday camp swimming pool, hit my head on the bottom, broke my neck and spent the next year at the world-famous Stoke Mandeville Hospital. As I have written elsewhere (Oliver, 1982), this was not a wholly negative experience, although, of course, things like having a metal frame screwed into my skull while fully conscious are not experiences I would want to repeat.

However, the positive far outweighed the negative. The culture of Stoke Mandeville was definitely macho, and I was encouraged to undertake as much physical activity, loosely called rehabilitation, as I wanted. Additionally, there were the women; nurses, physios, OTs, all of whom were in close proximity and many of whom were required to perform professional acts of intimacy. It is not surprising that the boundaries between these professional and personal acts of intimacy were often blurred in the evenings and at weekends, given that the majority of the patients were young men and the majority of the staff were young women.

I think I learned more about myself and personal relationships in the one year I spent there than I have subsequently in the thirty years or more I spent in another kind of institution, the university. But there were other important gains as well. My relationships with my parents and other family members grew stronger at a time when often for young people such relationships grow weaker as they strive for independence. On leaving hospital, my mates and the working-class community that I had left welcomed me back.

For a while, all was well. My life continued as it had before the accident, except that I did not have a boring clerical job to go to. Soon it became apparent that endless days without boring work were even more boring than endless days with it and, while my family remained close and supportive, I began to feel restless and that there must be more to life than watching television, being taken out by your mates and drinking. The next major change in my life occurred not because of the successful intervention of skilled professionals but purely by luck.

The personal and the professional

My professional interest in disability did not really come about until some ten years after I became disabled as the result of the spinal injury in 1962. After my year in Stoke Mandeville Hospital, I spent three years unemployed and thinking I was unemployable – a perception that was reinforced by every single professional I met during that time. In 1966, purely by chance, I was offered a job as a clerk at the young offenders' prison near where I lived.

Despite my previous boring experience as a clerk I was persuaded by the charismatic principal of the education centre in the prison that this was a great opportunity. I did not need much persuading and within a matter of months the not-so-boring clerical job had changed and I became a lecturer in the education centre of the same establishment and remained there for six years. However, being unqualified, in 1972 I went to university and read for a degree in sociology. On completion, I remained for a further three years to undertake research and gain my doctorate.

As a postgraduate student, my interests were in the fields of deviance and crime rather than illness and disability. The positivist view dominated the academic world at this time; according to this, one did not become involved in subjects in which one had a personal involvement or interest because this made objectivity very difficult, if not impossible. However, as a postgraduate student with a young family to support, one of the few occasions when disability became a positive advantage was when the Open University began looking for course tutors for its new disability course. In addition, in my own research I was exploring the supposed links between crime and epilepsy (Oliver, 1979, 1980) and this inevitably meant that I had to read some medical sociology because epilepsy was conceptualized as illness rather than deviance. I quickly discovered that then, as now, many medical sociologists proceed on the assumption that illness and disability are the same thing. Despite several honourable attempts in recent years to bring the two sides of the divide together (Barnes and Mercer, 1996; Thomas, 1999), little progress towards a rapprochement has been made.

When I began to read some of the things that able-bodied academics, researchers and professionals had written, and still write, about impairment and disability, I was and remain staggered at how little it related to my own experience or, indeed, that of most other disabled people I had come to know. Over the next few years it gradually began to dawn on me that if disabled people left it to others to write about disability, we would inevitably end up with inaccurate and distorted accounts of our experiences and inappropriate service provision and professional practices based upon these inaccuracies and distortions. I would love to say that this has changed in recent years but regrettably it has not.

It was during the 1970s that women were beginning to reject male accounts of their experiences and black people were vehemently denying the accuracy of white descriptions of what it was like to be black. This questioning had reverberations throughout the academic world, calling into question the whole notion of objectivity and bringing subjectivity onto the academic agenda.

At this time, as a sociologist I found myself supporting the call for a committed and partisan sociology (Gouldner, 1975). As a disabled person I found myself empathizing with the position of feminists who saw 'objectivity as the word men use to talk about their own subjectivity' (Rich, quoted in Morris, 1992b). As a disabled sociologist I found myself in the 'academic disability ghetto' but determined to render an accurate, undistorted and wholly subjective account of disability. I have no regrets about being in the disability ghetto. It has enabled me to teach about disability issues to students at the universities of Kent and Greenwich, where I have worked as a full-time academic, as well as at a whole range of other assorted universities, polytechnics and colleges. As well as undergraduate and postgraduate students, I have been involved in both initial and post-qualifying training to professional groups, including social workers, teachers, nurses, occupational therapists and physiotherapists and doctors.

Before leaving this academic part of my biography, I need to return to my involvement with the Open University. In particular, its first course on disability issues, 'The Handicapped Person in the Community', had a key influence on my thinking. While it was based upon the assumptions that disability was a condition of the individual and that the way to deal with it was through professional interventions designed to deal with either the medical complications or functional limitations of impaired individuals, it nonetheless provided both an opportunity to read some of the academic literature on disability and an academic focus to take further my thinking on disability. In addition this involvement gave me the opportunity to work with Vic Finkelstein. While I knew Vic, and that he had had a key influence in the Union of the Physically Impaired Against Segregation (UPIAS) and on the *Fundamental Principles* document they published (1976), it was not until then that I realized the importance of the work we were beginning to undertake in redefining disability.

By the time the 'Handicapped Person' course came to be rewritten, we had both penned major critiques of the individual model of disability, as it came to be called (Finkelstein, 1980; Oliver, 1983), which saw all the problems that disabled people faced as being consequent on their impairments. These critiques had called into question the appropriateness of professional interventions based upon this model and the rewritten course was much more centrally concerned to create a partnership with professionals. In my own work I had established the first postgraduate course in what later came to be called 'Disability Studies' at the University of Kent. At this time I think Vic realized the importance of the work we were beginning to undertake in shaping the future of disability studies and indeed professional education, but for me it was much more about having a job and paying the mortgage.

As our understanding of disability issues grew the Open University produced a completely new course entitled 'The Disabling Society', reflecting these changes. By now disability had been redefined by many disabled people and their representative organizations as the social barriers, restrictions and/or oppressions they face and professional interventions have come to be seen as often adding to these problems rather than seeking to deal with them. These changes are, therefore, a part of my own personal biography for, in one way or another, I have been involved in these courses almost since the beginning, initially as a course tutor and then as a member of the course team for the rewrite and production of the new course.

Hence, it would not be inaccurate to say that changes in my own thinking about disability were both reflected in and influenced by changes in the OU and Kent courses. By the 1990s, the fledgling disability studies had flown the nest and courses began to appear elsewhere, notably at Leeds and Sheffield. And later, following my own appointment as the first UK professor of disability studies, a number of similar chairs were created to support these initiatives. Hopefully they have had some effect on the way others have thought about disability, among them disabled people and professionals in particular. I will discuss disability studies further elsewhere in this book, notably in the final chapter.

The personal becomes the political

To return to my own developing consciousness of disability issues, my original attitude was one that is not uncommon among disabled people today. It can perhaps be best characterized by the term 'denial'; not denial as it is usually seen by professionals, that is, as a pathological response to my own impairment, but a denial of the fact that I might have anything in common with other disabled people. So I actively sought to avoid contact with other disabled people wherever possible, either on the street or by joining organizations.

This avoidance was only partial, however, because prior to my accident I had been a keen sportsman and my interest remained. Hence, for many years I participated in what were then called the 'Stoke Mandeville Games', at both national and international level. While I think the value of sport for disabled people is overstated in therapeutic and rehabilitative terms, there is no doubt that it was valuable to me personally; it enabled me to maintain a positive self-identity, it made my denial only partial and it embedded me in a network of social relationships, many of which remain today.

It also provided me with my first experience of collective action. There was a move to exclude tetraplegics from some of the more prestigious international events because it was argued that their needs for personal assistance were too great. The real truth was that providing personal assistants to disabled people would have drastically reduced the places available for the hangers-on who bedevil all sports. A few of us organized ourselves and mobilized support from other competitors and the plan was quickly dropped, publicly at least. The victory was only partial, of course, because behind the scenes machinations continued to exclude some of us but the experience of political action was an empowering one, even if I did not see it as political at the time.

Around this time I was also trying to acquire the educational qualifications I had missed out on as a working-class failure of the grammar school system, and this was proving no easy matter. Poor access to educational buildings coupled with the disablist attitudes of many educators meant that a thick skin was a necessary prerequisite for kicking open the door of educational opportunity. I soon realized that if that door was not only to be kicked open for those individuals powerful enough to do so, but also was to remain open, individual action could never be enough.

As my undergraduate career was coming to an end, I heard of an initiative to keep this door permanently open by creating an organization that became the National Bureau for Handicapped Students (NBHS), later to rebrand itself as SKILL, as many outdated organizations tend to do. I attended the inaugural conference and eagerly joined its council of management. At the same time, there was a move to form an impairment specific self-help group for people with spinal injuries. Again I attended the inaugural meeting, and as soon as my studies permitted, I joined the management committee of the Spinal Injuries Association.

Over the next few years, my experiences of collective action in these two groups differed radically. SIA was controlled by disabled people, it knew its mission was to represent people with a spinal injury and it was not afraid to speak out, tread on toes or offend vested interests. I was never sure who controlled NBHS but I quickly came to realize that its (unspoken) mission was to protect the interests of educational establishments and the staff who worked in them; it rarely spoke out on anything and most of the vested interests were represented on its council of management.

As a result I left NBHS in disillusion after a few years, but remained with SIA for sixteen. Furthermore, these experiences left me convinced that only organizations controlled by disabled people could properly represent the wishes of disabled people. My own personal experience had convinced me of something of general importance and I found support for this in the sociological literature.

> Social theories are grounded in the knowledge the theorist has gained through personal experience. Facts, rooted in personal reality, are of course utterly persuasive to the theorist. He becomes involved in, sees, experiences, such things as the French Revolution, the rise of socialism, the great Depression, and he never doubts the factuality of his experience. (Gouldner, 1975, p. 70)

As Gouldner concludes, I have not since doubted the factuality of that experience. Nor indeed have I had cause to; I have not since encountered a non-representative, non-democratic organization that properly addresses, let alone represents, the collective interests of disabled people. Thus, when there was a move to form a cross-impairment, national coordinating organization of disabled people, I used whatever power and influence I had within SIA to ensure they fully backed it. The British Council of Organizations of

Disabled People (BCODP) duly emerged and has gone from strength to strength; more will be said in this regard in later chapters. The point here is that, with the emergence of the BCODP, my personal journey from individual denial to the collective embracement of disabled people was complete.

However, the world does not stand still and, although I retained some involvement with BCODP for many years, when I retired I retired from everything. While I remain as committed as ever to the disabled people's movement, the world of disability politics has not stood still. Many of the big charities have attempted to rebrand themselves, like SKILL, and have convinced ignorant governments and other funders that they are an integral part of what they like to call the disability movement. BCODP itself has been less effective partly as a consequence of this and has even gone through its own rebranding exercise, emerging as the United Kingdom Council of Disabled People (UKCDP).

If this shift in power away from organizations of disabled people and back to the big charities continues then, in my view, the future for disabled people in the twenty-first century will be bleak. I remember what it was like trying to build a decent life for myself and my family when there were only the big charities around. I also remember just how empowering it was when I had the collective strength of other disabled people around me. I'm glad that I'm not trying to build a decent life for myself in the here and now and I'm scared about whether I will be able to hang on to the life I've got as I continue to age. But perhaps I worry too much and the collective power of the big charities will save me and the thousands of other disabled people currently going through the same experience.

The personal is the political

So far, my description of my journey towards understanding has been rooted in events that happened in my life. There is a more personal aspect of the journey, however, which is about the transformation of my own consciousness of disability from personal trouble to political issue. Kickstarting the transformation from the personal to the political is a problem. For me it was resolved not by becoming active in left politics, which is the traditional way for working-class children, but rather through listening to the music of Bob Dylan. His descriptions of injustice, inequality and moral outrage in his early songs had a far greater impact on the development of my political consciousness than did my working-class background.

While this exposure led to a growing political awareness, it was a generalized awareness only. The links to the politics of disability were non-existent at this time; there were no disabled role models, heroes and heroines who could link my growing awareness of inequalities and injustice, and my own growing sense of moral outrage, to my experience as a disabled person, nor, indeed, to the experience of disabled people generally. Of course, impaired role models existed in large numbers – heroes and heroines as well as victims and villains: Douglas Bader, Beethoven, Julius Caesar, Richard III, Mr Magoo and many more (Rieser and Mason, 1990; Barnes, 1992). However, none of these role models made sense of my own experience as a disabled person. I felt neither heroic nor victimized, I was neither brave nor pathetic and I certainly did not see myself as a villain, made bitter and twisted by my impairment. But I was beginning to realize that my experiences as a disabled person had a political as well as a personal dimension.

The connections between disability and politics, however, were not easy to make. It was almost as if they were deliberately kept in different cognitive spheres. Even where there were specific links between politics and disability in the lives of individual disabled people, these links were often deliberately covered up. For example, the two most famous impaired Americans were probably Franklin Delano Roosevelt and Helen Keller. He became president but most people did not even know he had an impairment; she was known for being deaf and blind but hardly anyone knew or now knows she was a committed socialist who strongly supported the Russian Revolution and the government that came after it, when it was far from safe to do so in America.

The links between politics and disability in these two cases raise interesting questions – a politician whose impairment is denied and a disabled person whose politics is denied. It is difficult to decide which is the most unfortunate. In Britain, on the other hand, there are some disabled politicians who neither deny their impairments nor their politics. The problem is that they don't see the connection between the two and they fail to embrace their impairments as part of a politics of personal identity.

An example of this was the Special Award for Word Blindness that the Greater Manchester Coalition of Disabled People gave to David Blunkett, then Shadow Minister for Health and a blind person, on the grounds that 'since his arrival at Westminster and promotion to the Shadow Cabinet [he] has never been heard to speak those immortal words "disabled people"' (*Coalition*, December 1993). Even when the Labour Party came into power in 1997 and he occupied some key positions in government, he continued to show his ignorance of 'real' disability politics. Since his fall from grace, little has changed. The British Prime Minister Gordon Brown, on the other hand, follows a different path. Though he has a visual impairment you wouldn't know it, either from his self-identity or his political 'convictions'.

Two of my own heroes, Antonio Gramsci and Woodrow Wilson Guthrie, were impaired but would not have understood these impairments as part of a politics of personal identity either. One died, imprisoned in Mussolini's jails for his political views, the other died imprisoned in his own head because of Huntington's Chorea. Neither saw his impairment as an essential part of self. Neither saw his politics as influenced by the personal restrictions he experienced as a consequence of his impairment. This, I suppose, is not surprising if you're confronted with the social restrictions imposed by fascist police, racist rednecks or anti-union thugs.

In my striving to relate my personal experiences of impairment to the social restrictions of disability, I found few disabled heroes in fiction, television or film. As far as writing is concerned, where impairment or disability does feature, it is usually seen as personal tragedy (Rieser and Mason, 1990). Where disabled people have written about themselves, it has all too often been within the 'how I overcame my impairment/disability' genre. Film and television provided, and continue to provide, a mass of super-cripple and emotionally stunted disabled stereotypes. In recent years, however, largely due to the influence of the disabled people's movement on film or television, a few candidates for hero-worship are beginning to emerge.

My own personal favourite is paraplegic ex-war hero Luke Martin, played by Jon Voight in the film *Coming Home*, which was first shown in 1978; not just because of what he did to Jane Fonda, but also because his personal disillusionment with the Vietnam War and its aftermath drove him to chain himself to the gates of an army recruiting station. In him, the personal nearly becomes the political, but not quite. His protest was an individual one and thus ultimately doomed to failure. He may have saved himself but the disabling society lives on; the USA continues to fight imperialistic wars in the name of freedom and by so doing continues to create impaired people in their thousands.

While there may be emerging a variety of role models which will enable impaired people to understand their personal experiences in political terms, there still remains the problem that the cultural discourse on disability remains structured by the tragedy principle (Hevey, 1992). The 'triumph over tragedy' principle still rules the mass media in newspapers, books and films and disabled people are constantly stereotyped as heroic victims or embittered villains. The complexities of the way impairment interacts with other personal characteristics are barely considered and, among disabled people, this may be worse for some than others:

> Ask yourselves, when you last saw a film or television drama or soap with a lesbian or gay relationship at the centre of the story? . . . Far from pulverising you with lesbian and gay material – we are deprived of personal, political and cultural representation! . . . This cultural and informational deprivation is imposed BY A SOCIETY THAT TAKES LITTLE OR NO ACCOUNT OF THE NEEDS OF lesbians and gay men! Where have I heard something like that before? (Gillespie-Sells, 1993, p. 24)

With films like *Brokeback Mountain*, among others, this may no longer be the case, but such offerings don't portray the needs of disabled lesbians and disabled gay men.

There are non-disabled real-life heroes who helped me to link the personal with the political. For me, Muhammad Ali was not just the greatest boxer who ever lived but also one of the most important figures of the twentieth century. He embraced black pride, confronted religious bigotry and combined this with an opposition to the most obscene war in the history of humankind at great personal and financial cost. For him it was not just a matter of the personal being the political but, equally importantly, the political being the personal. He would not fight in Vietnam because he saw it as the white race making war on others. He also knew about the importance of being called by the name he wanted and he vigorously resisted being named by others, something that is also important to disabled people.

Two of my other heroes, Tommie Smith and John Carlos, used personal triumphs to make political statements. Having won a gold and bronze medal respectively at the Olympic Games in Mexico City in 1968, both men stood on the victory rostrum and raised their black-gloved hands in victory salute. In so doing, both knew they were giving up the potential riches that white society would offer if they sold out. To this day both have remained true to the beliefs that underpinned this gesture and work within black communities in their struggles against racism.

It is not all heroes or leaders who remain true to their communities. Working-class movements have been bedevilled by leaders who became part of the bourgeoisie; black movements have encountered similar problems, naming the black bourgeoisie as 'uncle Toms'. Disabled people have a similar word for their bourgeoisie – 'tiny Tims'. This stems from Charles Dickens' use of the disabled child character tiny Tim in his novel *A Christmas Carol*. Tiny Tim was portrayed as pitiful and ultimately became the beneficiary of a rich man's charity: a position not unfamiliar to some disabled people these days.

Over the years we have seen media stories of disabled people climbing mountains, trekking in jungles or across polar icecaps and sailing the stormy seas. In order to do so they are happy to reinforce stereotypical media imagery of disabled people and become the modern day 'tiny Tims' in the eyes of other disabled people who feel such imagery should be challenged rather than embraced.

Many of these charitable exploitations have become institutionalized now; in the USA they have 'the telethon' and in Britain we have *Children in Need*. Through no fault of their own, many of these children are coerced into becoming modern-day versions of tiny Tim.

Since writing the first edition of this book, I would like to say that new heroes have emerged to shape my disability consciousness further, but regrettably this has not been the case. There are three reasons for this I think: first, events in the world have changed considerably and recent years have seen the re-emergence of many villains on the world stage; second, the media in all its forms has moved on from its interest in disability issues, although it claims to have incorporated these issues into its mainstream agenda; and, third, my own retreat from academic and public life has been accompanied by a change in my own interests and there is not the space here to write about some of my current heroes, such as 'Roy the Boy', 'Crazy Horse', 'Dodger Mcartney' or 'Eddie the Shoe'.

The personal is still the personal, after all

For a number of reasons, 1996 was a pivotal year for me. Professionally, I had published the first edition of this book and one on the history of the disabled people's movement with Jane Campbell (Campbell and Oliver, 1996). The Sociology Department at Greenwich had undergone two successful government assessments, one for teaching and one for research. I was in demand to speak at international conferences and to provide lucrative consultancy services to a variety of different organizations and some of my earlier work was being translated into several different languages. In my personal life, I was very happily married for a second time. My two children had left home, though, as many parents will confirm, they never really leave. And for the first time in my working life, I had money left over at the end of each month rather than being in debt.

However, there was a downside to all this as well. In terms of my writing, I felt that there was little more I wanted to say. In terms of research, the only projects I was interested in undertaking weren't fundable at the time, though government agendas now appear to have changed at least in terms of the language they use. Sociology was suffering a slow decline in popularity for two reasons: the competition from psychology and criminology fuelled by the popularity of television crime series; and many sociologists were embracing postmodernism and/or retreating into philosophy. Internally, the universities were changing to accommodate government demands for accountability and greater productivity, making them much less friendly places to work. All this left me looking for a way out, though it was not until 2002 that my university and I came to a satisfactory agreement about this.

Personally, I had no wish to work until I exhausted myself to the point where I was unable to enjoy my retirement. I had seen my father do this out of financial necessity and I was fortunate not to be in the same situation. I was also becoming increasingly aware that, as I aged with my impairment, my abilities to live a full and demanding life needed more attention and that I needed to make regular changes to the way I managed it. Not only that, but also, psychologically, I came to feel that I was no longer able to take things in my life for granted as I previously had and this led to periodic panic or anxiety attacks. So when my university eventually decided to make me a reasonable early retirement offer I was delighted to accept.

In trying to understand the journey of my life myself, the black-and-white film *The Incredible Shrinking Man* provided a key to my understanding. In it the hero, Scott Carey, is contaminated by a radioactive cloud combined with pesticide and from that point he starts to shrink. I remember watching it with my children on television when they were very small and they were terrified when Carey fought a life and death battle with a very large spider armed only with a pin. I was terrified too by the film but it took me many years and the help of a real 'shrink' to understand why. The story mirrors all of our lives: we come from infinity and grow continuously to the point where we start shrinking until we again disappear into infinity.

It feels like I started shrinking in 1996 at precisely the point in my personal and professional life were 'as good as it gets', but, despite this, panic and anxiety attacks were becoming a problem for me. Not everyone reacts to their own shrinking in the same way that I did, however. Some accept it and grow old gracefully; others rage against 'the dying of the light' and still others ignore it and continue as if they're still growing. Personally, I hope that I'm in the first camp because I've always been against the triumph over tragedy frameworks used to interpret people's reactions to impairment, chronic illness or impending death. The film also helps me to understand why my favourite Leonard Cohen song is 'Dance Me'. It is also about the journey of our lives and certainly there are echoes of mine in it in the line:

> 'Dance me through the panic til I'm gathered safely in.'
> (Lyrics by Leonard Cohen
> Copyright © 1992 Sony/ATV Music Publishing
> All rights reserved used by permission.)

So where am I on the journey of my life? Well, I'm still shrinking but I'm also still dancing, as I hope the rest of this book will demonstrate.

Conclusion

The purpose of this revised chapter has been to show how my own developing consciousness – my personal biography, my attempts to theorize about disability, my growing involvement with the disabled people's movement and, finally, my gradual retreat from the political to the personal – have shaped my thinking about the rest of the things you will read about in this book. I hope that the road map you now have from the Introduction and the window you have on my life from this chapter will serve you well in trying to understand what follows and that you won't end up wasting your time.

2

Mobility Impairment in a Social Context

This chapter reproduces my Inaugural Professorial Lecture from 1993 and was published as Chapter 7 of the first edition of this book. I have reproduced it here for three reasons: first, the fact that I have had a mobility impairment for more than forty-five years has been of central importance in my life; second, my professorial lecture was an important landmark in my academic career; and, third, it shows that the claims that my work ignores impairment are false. I was tempted to update it but decided against because, despite the changing world, it still captures my essential views about the issues that I address therein.

In the first part of that lecture I examined our cultural assumptions about walking by focusing on its representation in popular songs. I was tempted to look at popular music over the last twenty years but quickly realized that I knew absolutely nothing about this music, and attempts to persuade my grandchildren to act as unpaid researchers were treated with the disdain they probably deserved. Along the way I have turned one of them onto the music of Bob Dylan, but that's another story only mentioned here because it is one of my proudest achievements.

The second part of the lecture sent up some of the medical research charities as millenarian movements, although they didn't seem to think it was very funny. I am delighted to report, however, that since then their claims about the imminence of 'cures' have become much more muted. I would like to suggest that this is due to me, but it is much more likely to be down to the fact you can only claim for so long that a cure for this or that impairment is just round the corner without losing your credibility and, more importantly, your ability to continue to raise funds.

There have been two exceptions to this. The first was the media hysteria created around 'Superman' Christopher Reeve, from the time he became paralyzed until his death. Accordingly, he became the superhero battling to cure disabled people throughout the world, even though many don't want to be cured and some of those that do resented the way the issues were portrayed. The reality was that he was seeking it for himself and died long before his own 'kryptonite cure' arrived. The second exception occasionally occurs when unscrupulous research scientists are coming to the end of their grants and issue upbeat press releases, which are picked up by lazy journalists. This sometimes results in tomorrow's front-page headlines, but soon becomes the next day's fish-and-chip paper.

In the third part of the lecture I focused on rehabilitation and its obsession with walking. We have seen a shift away from this to some extent, although, again, I cannot claim that my lecture was responsible. The relative success of the independent living movement in redefining what disabled people mean by independence has been much more influential, even if its success at obtaining appropriate services and support has been much more limited.

~~~~~~~~~~

What's so wonderful about walking?

Introduction

It is, perhaps, perverse to choose as the focus for my professorial lecture an activity that I myself have not engaged in for more than thirty years. It may be, but it is also deliberate. It is to counter the criticism sometimes wrongly levelled at my work; namely that I privilege experience over methodology. In other words, that I believe that only disabled people should do disability research.

To say that research by able-bodied researchers has served disabled people badly, or indeed work by men has served women badly and work by whites has served black people badly, is not privileging experience over methodology. It is criticizing inaccurate, distorting and, at times, downright oppressive sociological research dominated by white, able-bodied males. Hence, I hope to demonstrate that a non-walker can make a significant contribution to our understanding of walking, both sociologically and anthropologically and without distorting the experience of walkers.

Before going on to develop this further, I should include a cautionary note about the political correctness of the terminology I shall be using. I am well aware that 'disabled people' is the politically correct term for describing the people I will be discussing, but I am going to put that aside for the purposes of this lecture. As walking is the central, organizing concept of the discussion, I am going to divide the world into walkers, non-walkers and nearly-walkers.

The time to discuss the political correctness or incorrectness of this classification may be when I have finished, but if I offend any disabled people, then I apologize in advance. If I offend any academics, researchers or professionals who have wrongly categorized us or distorted our experience with their schemes, then now you know how it feels.

Finally, I should add that walking is an appropriate topic for my professorial lecture, for as a young academic, the very first paper I ever had published was on this subject, in the *International Journal of Medical Engineering and Technology*. For a sociologist this was no small feat. Having reread this paper recently when preparing this lecture, I was pleasantly surprised to find how much I still agreed with; so much so that I was tempted to merely reproduce it as the lecture and then confess at the end.

However, while that might have been a clever trick, it would not have shown how my own understanding of walking has developed over the years and the role that sociology has played in this development. So, for those of you bursting to know how clever and insightful I was all those years ago, you will have to be satisfied with the following quote, unless you want to read the original yourself: '[T]he aim of research should not be to make the legless normal, whatever that may mean, but to create a social environment where to be legless is irrelevant' (Oliver, 1978, p. 137). While I cringe, some fifteen years later, at the political incorrectness of some of my terminology, I still agree with the sentiment behind it.

I would not want to pretend that, following such seminal insights, such a thing as the sociology of walking has sprung up or even that sociologists have been queuing up to study the topic in the way that they have other more sexy topics like class, or deviance, or medicine, or more recent discoveries like race and gender. However, the sociology of the body has become sexy recently and one of its leading theorists,

Bryan S. Turner, made a throwaway comment on walking in one of
his attempts to theorize the body. He wrote:

> Walking is a capacity of the biological organism, but it is also a human creation
> and it can be elaborated to include the 'goose-step', the 'march', and 'about-
> turn'. Walking is rule-following behaviour, but we can know a particular
> person by his walk or by the absence of a walk. . . . my way of walking may
> be as much a part of my identity as my mode of speech. Indeed, the 'walk' is
> a system of signs so that the stillness of the migrainous person or the limp of
> the gouty individual is a communication. (Turner, 1984, p. 236)

What for him was a throwaway comment, I take as the starting
point for this lecture. Walking is not merely a physical activity which
enables individuals to get from place a to place b. It is also a symbolic
act, but not merely symbolic as far as individuals are concerned; it
is also culturally symbolic and therefore it is necessary to understand
walking sociologically, given that a central problematic of sociology is
to understand 'the meaning of life'.

I do not intend here to provide 'the' or even 'a' sociology of walking,
nor do I intend to sketch out an agenda for what a sociology of walking
might look like. Instead, I shall apply some sociological ideas to the
issue of walking and see how far that gets us. In so doing, I shall focus
on three areas: the meaning of walking at the cultural level; the pursuit
of the idea of walking as a millenarian rather than medical activity;
and the influence of the ideology of walking on the enterprise of
rehabilitation. Finally, I shall address some remarks to the purpose of
this, or, to quote the words of a currently unfashionable sociologist
called Lenin, 'What is to be done?'

Walking and culture

In considering the meaning of walking at the cultural level, I have
decided to concentrate on its cultural production within the realms of
the popular song, not simply because it is something I have a passing
interest in, but because popular songs tell us more about the meaning
of life than do other more elitist cultural forms such as squawking in a
foreign language, jumping around on stage by over-muscled men and
anorexic women or reading Sunday-supplement novels.

My interest in the relationship between popular song and walking
was awakened by a remark made by David Swift, a nearly-walker who
appeared on the recent Channel 4 series on the history of disability. As

a nearly-walker, he was reflecting on his ability or inability to attract girls in the dance halls of Nottingham in the 1950s:

> I didn't have many girlfriends, more casual acquaintances. Once they got to know the way I walked ... I mean there were plenty of songs coming out where they say, 'Look at the way she walks'. Everything was 'He walks like an angel ... Just walking in the rain ... Walking my baby back home'. And I'm thinking to myself about all these songs related to walking. And I couldn't even walk properly. What had I got to show? But I found the key pretty early. I found the key to getting a girl was to play the fool. I'd got to get their eyes away from my legs. So as long as I could keep them laughing I was alright. But as soon as I saw their eyes lowering, I knew the danger was coming. (Humphreys and Gordon, 1992, p. 114)

Perhaps the song that says it all is one by Val Doonican called 'Walk Tall', which contains the refrain:

> Walk tall, walk straight and look the world right in the eye,
> that's what my momma told me when I was about knee high.
> She said, son be a proud man and hold your head up high,
> walk tall, walk straight and look the world right in the eye.

Though, I don't know for sure, I like to think that when Lois Keith made her poetic attack on the sexist and ambulist nature of language, she had that song in mind. For those of you who don't know it, this is her poem:

> Tomorrow I am going to re-write the English language
> I will discard all those striving ambulist metaphors
> Of power and success
> And construct new images to describe my strength
> My new, different strength.
> Then I won't have to feel dependent
> Because I can't Stand On My Own Two Feet
> And I will refuse to feel a failure
> Because I didn't Stay One Step Ahead.
> I won't feel inadequate
> When I don't Stand Up For Myself
> or illogical because I cannot
> Just Take It One Step at a Time.
> I will make them understand that it is a very male way
> To describe the world
> All this Walking Tall

And Making Great Strides.
Yes, tomorrow I am going to re-write the English
Language,
Creating the world in my own image.
Mine will be a gentler, more womanly way
To describe my progress.
I will wheel, cover and encircle
Somehow I will learn to say it all.
(Keith, 1994)

Popular songs do not simply dismiss non-walkers or nearly-walkers in symbolic or metaphorical terms. The classic of the genre is the Kenny Rogers hit, which features the paralyzed veteran of some 'crazy, Asian war' pleading with his wife not 'to take her love to town'. It contains my favourite lyric in the whole of popular music, 'It's hard to love a man whose legs are bent and paralyzed'. So, non-walkers and nearly-walkers are not simply socially inadequate, they are sexually incompetent as well.

I know, just as one swallow doesn't make a summer, a few lyrics from one cultural form are not the whole story, but as more and more disabled people are subjecting other cultural forms to critical analysis, the full picture of just how disablist our culture really is is beginning to emerge. But to stay unapologetically within the cultural form I have chosen, as Lesley Gore once sang, 'It's my party and I'll cry if I want to' so 'It's my lecture and I'll say what I want to'.

Walking and cure

The pursuit of restoring the ability to walk or nearly walk is better understood, I would argue, as a millenarian movement rather than as the logical application of modern medical knowledge. For those of you unclear what such a movement is, I offer the following definition: 'In sociology, a millenarian movement is a collective, this-worldly movement promising total social change by miraculous means' (Abercrombie, Hill and Turner, 1988, p. 157). In Britain, I would argue, a number of such movements currently exist, exclusively, or almost exclusively, to solve the 'problem' of non-walking or nearly walking. They call themselves charities and they raise and spend probably in excess of £100 million pounds in pursuit of cures for what they usually call 'chronic or crippling diseases' every year.

It could, and usually is, argued that these are organizations devoted to the pursuit of scientific research, and they cannot even be conceived of as millenarian movements awaiting the second coming, the arrival of the inter-galactic spaceships, the return of long-dead ancestors and the like.

The problem is, of course, that throughout the history of humankind, the number of cures that have been found to these 'chronic and crippling diseases' could be counted on the fingers of one hand and still leave some over to eat your dinner with. And in empirical terms, there are considerably more examples of 'so-called' miraculous cures, than there are of those produced by scientific medicine. Finally, creating a society where all non-walkers and nearly-walkers walked properly would indeed require total social change.

Can you imagine it? Architects could let their imaginations run riot and design buildings without worrying about access; employers could recruit whoever they wanted without considering disabled applicants; the problem of integrating disabled children would disappear; and all those professionals currently employed in 'looking after' disabled people would be out of work – revolutionary social change indeed!

If we take one example with which I am familiar and in which I have a personal interest, then perhaps it will become even clearer. The example is the International Spinal Research Trust and an anthropological case study of it might look like the following:

A prophet wandered the land (Britain) and he had a vision; that all those who had a spinal injury would one day be able to walk again. Not only that but that this vision could be achieved within five years if certain things were done. These included a range of behaviours and rituals and necessitated forming an organization to support them. He wandered the land and spoke to people of both high and low status, those afflicted and those not and convinced some that his vision was true. So the organization was formed.

But this was the beginning, not the end. In order for his vision to be achieved a number of rituals had to be performed and repeated. These included persuading the great and the good to get dressed in their finest clothes, go to places of high social status, drink too much alcohol, jump up and down and throw money at a table strategically placed at the end of the room. Those of lower social status performed rituals of a different kind, usually involving cutting holes in the tops of tins and then accosting non-believers in the street and demanding that they place money in them. Even the afflicted were expected to participate, either by inviting people to their houses, offering them coffee and then charging them extortionate prices for it or by pushing their wheelchairs right round the island to end up in exactly the same place they had started from.

This was not the end of the rituals, however, for the organization then collected all this money and passed it on to a group of men of special status, who wore white coats who worked in places called laboratories. These men then proceeded to buy or breed thousands of animals who were then ritually slaughtered. These men in white coats then meticulously recorded these activities and wrote about them for other men in white coats who could not be present while the rituals were being performed.

However, despite religiously following these rituals for the appointed time period, the vision did not materialize in the time period specified, the original prophet was forced to flee the land to an island on the other side of the world (Australia). Whether he is still having visions is unknown. The sect did not, however, disintegrate at this point, but continues today, still urging its believers to intensify their rituals and, indeed, blaming them for the 'failure of prophecy'.

In case you think that my description is (too) subjective, which of course it is, as is all anthropology and, indeed, sociology too, then I reproduce a statement from the current research director of the movement, responding to criticisms of their claims made by another organization representing people with a spinal injury, the Spinal Injuries Association (SIA):

> The criticisms in the SIA magazine were against a claim made in 1986 that a cure was realisable within 5 years. Given that this claim was hedged with the proviso that enough money had to be available, I still claim that it was not irresponsible ... I still believe that the timing is not impossible. There can be no certainty that a model of cure can be constructed in the laboratory by the end of 1992, but progress on the repair of damaged tracts has been so swift that it should not be ruled out. (Banyard, 1991)

This quote contains all the elements that characterize the response of millenarian movements when prophecy fails. First, the timeframe was elastic, not absolute. Second, the message was misunderstood; it was not a cure that was promised but 'a model of cure in the laboratory'. Third, the rituals necessary to bring about the millennium were not properly followed; in this case, not enough money was raised.

It is not just nineteenth-century millenarian movements, like the Melanese cargo cults or the North American Indian ghost dance, that these charities have much in common with, but also twentieth-century religious sects. One such sect visited Britain last year and claimed that 'some will be moved by the power of God for the first time'. And when, of course, no one left their wheelchair and started to walk, it was because the message was misunderstood; people would be moved spiritually, not physically.

From the false prophets of religious evangelism, from the dashed hopes of cargo cultists, from the abandoned visions of the ghost dancers to the exaggerated claims of the impairment charities (Hevey, 1992), the idea of restoring the function of walking to those who cannot or have lost the ability to do it reigns supreme. It reigns supreme too in the enterprise of rehabilitation.

Walking and rehabilitation

Rehabilitation can be defined in many ways but what is certain is that a whole range of practices stem from the definition adopted; to paraphrase the old W.I. Thomas dictum, 'if people define situations as real, then they are real in their consequences'. This is not contentious but the central problem with rehabilitation is that none of the definitions adopted can be shown to be in accord with the experience of disability and none of the practices stemming from these definitions can be shown to work effectively. To put matters bluntly, all is not well in the enterprise of rehabilitation, whether it be rehabilitation professionals expressing their anxiety (Royal College of Physicians, 1986) or their victims, and I use the term advisedly, expressing their discontent (Oliver *et al.*, 1988; Beardshaw, 1988).

I shall argue that central to the problem of rehabilitation is the failure to address the issue of power and to acknowledge the existence of ideology; both good, reputable sociological concerns. Hence, for me, rehabilitation is the exercise of power by one group over another and, further, that exercise of power is shaped by ideology. The exercise of power involves the identification and pursuit of goals chosen by the powerful and these goals are shaped by an ideology of normality, which, like most ideologies, goes unrecognized, often by professionals and their victims alike.

More of this later, but let me further emphasize here that I am not suggesting that we can eradicate the influence and effects of power and ideology in rehabilitation, but that our failure to even acknowledge their existence gives rise to a set of social relations and a range of therapeutic practices that are disabling for all concerned, whether they be professionals employed in the provision of rehabilitation services or disabled people as recipients of these services.

Space will not permit a detailed, sustained and comprehensive critique of rehabilitation, so in order to illustrate my argument I shall focus on a topic at the heart of the rehabilitation enterprise and this lecture – that of walking. Rehabilitation constructs the concept of walking uncritically in that it is never analyzed or discussed except in technical terms – what surgical operations can we perform, what aids can we provide and what practices can we use to restore the function of walking? Walking is more complex and complicated than that, both as a physical act and, indeed, a social symbol, as I hope I have already demonstrated.

In terms set by the rehabilitation enterprise, walking is rule-following behaviour; not-walking is rule-ignoring, rule-flouting or even rule-threatening behaviour. Not-walking can be tolerated when individuals are prepared to undergo rehabilitation in order to nearly walk or to come to terms with their non-walking. Not-walking or rejecting nearly-walking as a personal choice is something different however; it threatens the power of professionals, it exposes the ideology of normality and it challenges the whole rehabilitation enterprise.

A classic example of the way the ideology of normality linked to an uncritical concept of walking informs rehabilitation practice is this description and analysis by a person with a spinal injury:

> The aim of returning the individual to normality is the central foundation stone upon which the whole rehabilitation machine is constructed. If, as happened to me following my spinal injury, the disability cannot be cured, normative assumptions are not abandoned. On the contrary, they are reformulated so that they not only dominate the treatment phase searching for a cure but also totally colour the helper's perception of the rest of that person's life. The rehabilitation aim becomes to assist the individual to be as 'normal as possible'.
>
> The result, for me, was endless soul-destroying hours at Stoke Mandeville Hospital trying to approximate to able-bodied standards by 'walking' with callipers and crutches. (Finkelstein, 1988, pp. 4–5)

Nor indeed would I want to argue that most rehabilitation victims reject the idea of walking. One disabled person who clearly didn't was Philip Olds, an ex-policeman who was shot while trying to prevent an armed robbery. According to Jenny Morris, 'As he put it, before his injury, "I was a motorcycle riding, fornicating, beat walking, criminal catching man – a bit of a cross between Telly Savalas and Dennis Waterman"' (Morris, 1992, p. 2). He couldn't accept not-walking or nearly walking and, encouraged by both national newspapers and television producers, he pursued the idea of walking with a commitment bordering on desperation. As the general public, we read about and watched his efforts to walk, or nearly walk, with baited breath. He failed. While Vic Finkelstein, the author of the first quote, is still around more than thirty years after rejecting nearly walking, Philip Olds took an overdose in 1986. One commentator said he had been 'pressed to death' (Davis, 1987).

Polarizing two such different examples is, of course, being selective but all attempts to understand the meaning of life, depend upon us selecting and interpreting. I do not claim that my interpretation is the only one but I do claim that it is a valid one, and I further claim that it says much about the way power operates in the rehabilitation enterprise, as well as much about the way the mass media operates currently.

Power, of course, is a slippery concept to define, let alone recognize in operation. According to Lukes (1974b), central to the operation of power in society is what is not placed on the political (with a small p) agenda. Hence, as I have already suggested, the questions that are not asked are as important for rehabilitation as are those that are. A central question that is never asked of rehabilitation is its links with social control.

Questions concerning the therapeutic nature and effectiveness of rehabilitation are often asked; questions concerning the way rehabilitation often forces impaired individuals to do things that they would not freely choose to do for themselves are almost never asked. Links between the whole rehabilitation enterprise and wider aspects of social control are also never asked; after all, the ideology of the therapeutic state is caring, not controlling.

There are two dimensions to the operation of power that are relevant to questions of control: power to control the individual body and power to control the social body. The connections between the two are encapsulated in the work of the French philosopher Michael Foucault, whose discussion of health care systems has been summarized as follows: 'An essential component of the technologies of normalisation is the key role they play in the systematic creation, classification and control of anomalies in the social body' (Rabinow, 1984, p. 21). The relevance of the work of a dead French philosopher to rehabilitation may not be immediately apparent, but if for 'technologies of normalisation', we read rehabilitation practices, then uncomfortable questions are raised. The quote might then look something like this. 'An essential component of the rehabilitation enterprise is the key role it plays in the systematic creation, classification and control of anomalies in the social body.' To put the point succinctly in the language of this lecture, the aim of rehabilitation is to encourage walking and nearly walking, and to control through therapeutic interventions, non-walkers and nearly-walkers, both individually and as a group.

Like power, ideology is at its most influential when it is invisible and the ideology of normality permeates throughout the whole of society, a society which, according to Nabil Shaban, is based on body fascism. And of course, body fascism affects the lives of more of us than merely non-walkers and nearly-walkers; women, for example, to name one not unimportant section of the population.

The ideology of normality permeates most rehabilitation practice, from paediatrics through rheumatology and onto geriatrics. One example of where it surfaces is the current 'success' of conductive education. Many disabled people are profoundly disturbed by the ideology underpinning conductive education, which I have likened to the ideology of Nazism (Oliver, 1989). Lest anyone should be unclear about what's wrong with conductive education, its pursuit of nearly walking to the detriment of family, social and community life for many disabled children can only be countenanced as therapeutic intervention.

If able-bodied children were taken from their local school, sent to a foreign country, forced to undertake physical exercise for all their waking hours to the neglect of their academic education and social development, we would regard it as unacceptable and the children concerned would rapidly come to the attention of the child protection mafia. But in the lives of disabled children (and adults too) anything goes as long as you call it therapeutic.

What can be pernicious about ideology is not simply that it enables these issues to be ignored but sometimes it turns them on their heads. Hence, conductive education is not regarded as child abuse but as something meriting social applause, as something to make laudatory television programmes about, as something worthy of royal patronage and, finally, as something that should be funded by government and big business alike. The reality, not the ideology, of conductive education, and indeed many other rehabilitation practices, is that they are oppressive to disabled people and an abuse of their human rights. We should not pretend it is any other way.

This critique should not be regarded as an attempt to throw out the baby as well as the bath water. Rather it is an attempt to force onto the agenda of the rehabilitation enterprise issues it has barely considered. It is my belief that properly addressing these issues will make rehabilitation a more appropriate enterprise for all concerned – not only will the bath water be clearer but the baby healthier as well.

At the end of the day, 'To "rehabilitate" rehabilitation (and other human service agencies), we need to "rehabilitate" ourselves' (Higgins, 1985, p. 221).

What is to be done

A similar point is made by Ken Davis when he says, 'We can elevate the act of walking to an importance higher than engaging in the struggle to create a decent society' (Davis, 1987, p. 4). The point is, as I hope I have demonstrated, that walking has a significance beyond merely the functional. If it did not have, why would society punish non-walkers for not walking?

After all, we do not punish non-flyers for not flying. In fact we do exactly the opposite. We spend billions of dollars, yen, deutschmarks and pounds every year providing non-flyers with the most sophisticated mobility aids imaginable. They are called aeroplanes. An aeroplane is a mobility aid for non-flyers in exactly the same way as a wheelchair is a mobility aid for non-walkers.

But that is not the end of it, we spend at least as much money to provide environments, usually called runways and airports, to ensure that these mobility aids can operate without hindrance. Further, hundreds of thousands of people are employed worldwide, in helping non-flyers to overcome their particular mobility difficulties. And, finally, in order to provide barrier-free environments for non-flyers, we trample on the rights of others, ignoring their pleas not to have their homes bulldozed, their sleep disrupted, or their countryside disturbed.

Non-walkers are treated in exactly the opposite way. Environments are often designed to exclude us, transport systems that claim to be public continue to deny us access and when we protest we are told there is no money. We are also told that giving us access to such systems would adversely affect the rights of others; journeys would take longer and would be more expensive for everyone. Perhaps a useful slogan for the next direct-action demonstration could be 'equal treatment for non-walkers and non-flyers'.

Of course, it could be argued that not walking and not flying are not the same kinds of non-activity; the former affects only a minority, albeit a substantial one, whereas the latter affects everyone. True, but the numbers of non-flyers who are provided with the mobility aids to enable them to fly are even smaller; in other words, in world population terms, flyers are a smaller minority than non-walkers and nearly-walkers. My point is essentially one concerning social justice; treat both groups equally, or at the very least, stop punishing non-walkers and nearly-walkers for not walking.

To conclude then, some of you may have been surprised not simply by what I have said, but also by the way I have attempted to substantiate what I have said. In the world in which we live today, there are few certainties; knowledge, or what counts as knowledge, is both contested and contestable, and objectivity has been rigorously and rightly attacked by the politics of subjectivity.

In both sociology and the study of disability, this is doubly true. So, do not reject my arguments out of hand; if you disagree, contest them. If you think my comments on both elitist and popular culture are unfair, give me non-disablist examples of where disability is handled sensitively. If you think my characterizing medical charities as millenarian movements is inappropriate, give me examples of where they have provided cures rather than promises. If you think my description of rehabilitation as control rather than therapy is inaccurate, give me examples of non-controlling rehabilitation.

If Jenny Morris is right when she says, 'Disabled people are increasingly challenging the attitude that says that if you cannot walk, then your life isn't worth living' (Morris, 1992a, p. 3), and I believe that she is, then that challenge faces us all. As Ken Davis put it, we have to put our struggle to create a decent society above our vain attempts to force non-walkers and nearly-walkers to walk. I hope in addressing the question of what's so wonderful about walking I have made a contribution to this struggle.

3

The Social Model: History, Critique and Response

The social model emerged from my encounter with the *Fundamental Principles* document (UPIAS, 1976) and the way it forced me to rethink my own experiences of impairment and disability. This chapter acknowledges this debt but there is not the space in this edition to include as much of the original document as I would like or I did in the first edition. I also reproduce a table illuminating the social model because, despite claims to the contrary, I still believe it has explanatory power for those coming new to the social model. The rest of the chapter is taken from a paper I gave at an ESRC-sponsored seminar organized by Colin Barnes at the University of Leeds in 2002, which was later turned into a chapter for publication. (Barnes and Mercer, 2004).

In this chapter, I want to argue that, as the title implies, in the last twenty years we have spent too much time talking about the social model and its usefulness and indeed its limitations and not devoted enough attention to actually implementing or attempting to implement it in practice. This criticism applies both to the disabled people active in the disabled people's movement and those academics who have been central to the ongoing progress of disability studies.

In order to develop this viewpoint, first, I will provide a brief history of the social model from my own personal perspective as someone who was centrally involved in its elaboration, almost from the beginning. Second, I will explore the main criticisms of the social model that have emerged from the movement and from disability studies. Third, I will examine examples of the application of the social model with which, in one way or another, I have been involved. I will focus primarily on a project undertaken with Birmingham City Council (Oliver and Bailey, 2002).

~~~~~~~~~~

If I had a hammer: the social model in action

The history of the social model

The starting point for the social model was the publication of the *Fundamental Principles of Disability* by the Union of the Physically Impaired Against Segregation (UPIAS, 1976), which was an organization whose membership was exclusive to disabled people. It stated that:

> In our view, it is society which disables physically impaired people. Disability is something imposed on top of our impairments by the way we are unnecessarily isolated and excluded from full participation in society. Disabled people are therefore an oppressed group in society. To understand this it is necessary to grasp the distinction between the physical impairment and the social situation, called 'disability', of people with such impairment. Thus we define impairment as lacking part of or all of a limb, or having a defective limb, organ or mechanism of the body; and disability as the disadvantage or restriction of activity caused by a contemporary social organisation which takes no or little account of people who have physical impairments and thus excludes them from participation in the mainstream of social activities. Physical disability is therefore a particular form of social oppression.
>
> From this social point of view it follows that the impoverishment of physically impaired people arises out of the fact that, as a group, we are excluded from the mainstream of social activities. In the final analysis the particular form of poverty principally associated with physical impairment is caused by our exclusion from the ability to earn an income on a par with our able-bodied peers, due to the way employment is organised. This exclusion is linked with our exclusion from participating in the social activities and provisions that make general employment possible. For example, physically impaired school children are characteristically excluded from normal education preparatory to work, we are unable to achieve the same flexibility in using transport and finding suitable housing so as to live conveniently to our possible employment, and so on. The need to make a full analysis of the organisation of society is most pressing as this leads to the very essence of disability and its poverty aspect. It is clear that our social organisation does not discriminate equally against all physical impairments and hence there arises the appearance of degrees of exclusion (degrees of disability). For example, people having mild visual impairments (wearing glasses) are doubtless not more impoverished than their visually unimpaired peers. Our social organisation does not exclude people using glasses to the same extent that it excludes people who are blind, or deaf, or cannot speak, or who have brain damage, or who use wheelchairs. Nevertheless, it is the same society which disables people whatever their type, or degree of physical impairment, and therefore there is a single cause within the organisation of society that is responsible for the creation of the disability of

physically impaired people. Understanding the cause of disability will enable us to understand the situation of those less affected, as well as helping us to prevent getting lost in the details of the degrees of oppression at the expense of focusing on the essence of the problem. (UPIAS, 1976, pp. 14–15)

This turned the understanding of disability completely on its head by arguing that it was not impairment that was the main cause of the social exclusion of disabled people but the way society responded to people with impairments.

My more detailed elaboration of the social model stemmed from attempts to apply this insight in practice: first, in training of social workers and, second, in the design and delivery of disability equality training. More precisely, it emerged out of a course that I was teaching at the time that was the first postgraduate course in what would now be called disability studies. This was based at the University of Kent and was aimed primarily at qualified social workers, although some occupational therapists and others including a few disabled people also enrolled. Essentially, I was trying to provide my students with a way of applying the idea that it was society and not people with impairments that should be the target for professional intervention and practice. This approach was first introduced to a wider audience at a Royal Association for Disability and Rehabilitation (RADAR) conference in 1982. Subsequently, it was advanced in my book *Social Work with Disabled People* (Oliver, 1983).

In recent years there has been a great deal of discussion about different models of disability and what they mean for disability politics, policy and services, as well as how adequate they are as an explanation for the experiences that disabled people have. We have seen the emergence of individual and social models, the medical model, the charity model, the welfare and administrative models among others (Finkelstein, 1993). As the person who invented the term 'the social model of disability', though not the ideas behind it, I find the arrival of all these different models confusing rather than helpful.

For my part, I prefer to understand disability in terms of two models: the individual and the social. Models are ways of translating ideas into practice and the idea underpinning the individual model was that of personal tragedy, while the idea behind the social model was that of externally imposed restriction. I do not deny the influence (some positive, some negative) of medicine, charity and welfare in the lives of disabled people but none of these offers a sufficient foundation for building a distinctive model of disability.

For too long the individual model of disability has dominated disability policy and service provision (Oliver, 1996b). Linked to this has been the medicalization of disability, which has tended to regard disabled people as 'having something wrong with them' and hence the source of the problem. This medicalization, underpinned by the individual model, has not delivered adequate services to disabled people who are widely given a low priority when placed against the competing needs of other groups. This is particularly surprising given that, according to the government's own figures, disabled people are a significant minority who make up nearly a fifth of the population. It was not until the arrival of the social model that the necessary radical change in direction of service provision began to be articulated.

The thorny issue of the distinction between illness and disability still has not gone away. Most medical sociologists and many who work within disability studies continue to argue that the problems disabled people face are the result of the interaction between illness and disability. For me, however, this remains the cause of much conceptual confusion and I am clear that illness and disability are not the same thing; illness is caused by disease and disability is caused by social organization. The problem arises when this distinction is not recognized because those who adopt an 'interactive' approach fail to distinguish between illness and impairment and they are often discussed as if they were the same thing.

But as I hope I have made clear in the more personal sections of this book, this is not to deny the realities of impairment in general or my own impairment in particular. My own impairment is a spinal cord injury, which does not make me ill *per se* but I do also sometimes become ill with the same range of illnesses as non-disabled people. These are not simply 'how many angels can dance on the head of a pin'-type arguments because they have practical implications. Most illnesses are treatable and even curable by medical interventions; most impairments are not curable; and all disability can be eradicated by changes to the way we organize society. The problem this creates, as I hope I made clear in the previous chapter, is that we spend too much time and money searching for non-existent cures and not enough removing disabling barriers from the world in which we live.

In the first edition of this book, I provided a table to illustrate differences between the individual and social model of disability, (see Table 3.1). I also made it crystal clear that the table was trying to simplify a complex reality that linked the two models and should be seen as such. This part of the original text is also reproduced because

Table 3.1 Disability models

The individual model	The social model
personal tragedy theory	social oppression theory
personal problem	social problem
individual treatment	social action
medicalization	self-help
professional dominance	individual and collective responsibility
expertise	experience
adjustment	affirmation
individual identity	collective identity
prejudice	discrimination
attitudes	behaviour
care	rights
control	choice
policy	politics
individual adaptation	social change

subsequently the table has been used in isolation to completely distort and misinterpret my work on the social model (Shakespeare, 2006):

> It should be noted that, like all tables, this one oversimplifies a complex reality and each item should be seen as the polar end of a continuum. Nevertheless, underpinning it is the fundamental distinction between impairment and disability as defined by UPIAS above. (Oliver, 1996b, p. 33)

I want to make three general points about the social model. First, it is an attempt to switch the focus away from the functional limitations of individuals with an impairment on to the problems caused by disabling environments, barriers and cultures. Second, it refuses to see specific problems in isolation from the totality of disabling environments: hence the problem of unemployment does not just entail intervention in the social organization of work and the operation of the labour market but also in areas such as transport, education and culture. Third, endorsement of the social model does not mean that individually based interventions in the lives of disabled people, whether they be based on medicine, rehabilitation, education or employment, are of no use or always counter-productive (Oliver, 1996a).

From a social model perspective, too much is invested in individually based interventions with ever-diminishing returns. As a consequence, modifications to environments tend to be neglected or under resourced, despite the greater potential benefits of such invest-ments. To put it simply, providing a barrier-free environment is likely to benefit not just those with a mobility impairment but other groups as well (e.g. mothers with prams and pushchairs, porters with trol-leys), whereas physical rehabilitation will only benefit those privileged enough to be able to access it. This is not a criticism of rehabilitation per se, but more a comment on the efficient use of scarce resources.

Additionally, the traditional voice for disabled people had been the big charities that are still largely run and controlled by non-disabled people. Government initiatives like the establishment of the now defunct Disability Rights Commission (DRC) and other disability quangos have done little to change this situation, although the number of organizations controlled and run by disabled people grew steadily at both local and national levels until recently. This trend has now been reversed and many of the big charities have re-established themselves, claiming to be the voice of disabled people and to endorse the social model. Later in the book I refer to these changes as the emergence of disabling corporatism.

From theory to practice

We can see how the social model might be applied in examining cur-rent welfare to work policies in respect of disabled people. There is universal agreement that disabled people do not have the same access to jobs as the rest of the population. Estimates of the unemployment rates among disabled people suggest that they are between two and five times more likely to be unemployed and that this huge discrepancy can-not be accounted for solely on the grounds of impaired performance. However, government policies are, by and large, targeted at equip-ping impaired individuals for the unchanging world of work rather than changing the way work is carried out in order that more people might access it. Hence, much greater resources are currently spent on employment rehabilitation, training and so on (individual model) rather than on removing the barriers to work or on attempting to prevent the labour market from operating in a discriminatory manner (social model).

For example, the UK government is promoting disabled people's inclusion in the paid labour market with policies to revise the bene-fits system, and make radical changes in the operation of the labour market. All these sound like social model solutions to the problem of the high unemployment rate among disabled people. However, when the government talks about mechanisms to implement these changes, it focuses on two things: a small number of special schemes and job coaches for individual disabled people. So while the government accepts that the problems are external to disabled people, its solutions target individual disabled people.

In the broadest sense, the social model of disability is about nothing more complicated than a clear focus on the economic, environmental and cultural barriers encountered by people who are viewed by others as having some form of impairment – whether physical, sensory or intellectual. The barriers disabled people encounter include inaccessible education systems, working environments, inadequate disability benefits, discriminatory health and social support services, inaccessible transport, houses and public buildings and amenities, and the devaluing of disabled people through negative images in the media – films, television and newspapers. Hence, the cultural environment in which we all grow up usually sees impairment as unattractive and unwanted. Consequently, parent's feelings towards, and treatment of, a child born with an impairment are dependent upon what they have learned about disability from the world around them. Moreover, people who acquire impairment later in life have already been immersed in the personal tragedy viewpoint and it is not, therefore, surprising that many of these individuals find it difficult to know how to respond in any other way.

The social model of disability does not ignore questions and concerns relating to impairment and/or the importance of medical and therapeutic treatments. It acknowledges that in many cases, the suffering associated with disabled lifestyles is due primarily to the lack of medical and other services. It is similarly recognized that for many people coming to terms with the consequences of impairment in a society that devalues disabled people and disabled lifestyles is often a personal tragedy. But the real misfortune is that our society continues to discriminate, exclude and oppress people with impairments.

As a consequence, in Britain, there began a remarkable growth in organizations of disabled people in the 1980s, along with the appearance of disability equality training. Furthermore, the social model became the primary means of taking forward the idea of disability equality, across a whole range of trainers and organizations. The next stage in its development came when the disabled people's movement, notably the British Council of Organizations of Disabled People (BCODP), adopted the social model. If you read the book by Jane Campbell and myself, *Disability Politics: Understanding Our Past, Changing Our Future* (Campbell and Oliver, 1996), you will see quite clearly that it played a crucial role in enhancing the collective consciousness of disabled people and the emergence of the disabled people's movement (Campbell and Oliver, 1996).

But it was not just among disabled people that the social model idea gained recognition. It gradually became incorporated into the state and there were a number of reports, the first in 1988 was called *A Wider Vision for the Blind* (DHSS, 1988), which advocated the idea of the social model as the way forward in providing services for blind people. Thus, by the 1990s the social model was being colonized by a range of organizations, interests and individuals, some of whom had bitterly opposed its appearance less than ten years previously.

Criticisms of the social model

There are five main criticisms of the social model that have come from within the disabled people's movement and disability studies. The first of these is that the social model ignores or is unable to deal adequately with the realities of impairment. This is based upon a conceptual misunderstanding because the social model is not about the personal experience of impairment but the collective experience of disablement (Oliver, 1996b). This critique has sometimes turned into personal attacks and a few have suggested that it is only fit, white men in wheelchairs who are able to ignore their impairments.

As a severely disabled tetraplegic, who every day of my life needs to make the necessary arrangements to be able to get up in the morning and go to bed at night and, indeed, use the toilet, I find such suggestions galling, particularly when they come from non-disabled people or those disabled people who have no idea what it is like to be at the mercy of state services for personal survival, let alone social functioning. Of course, white men in wheelchairs are aware of the limitations that impairments impose, and of course we struggle with the difficulties they create for us. But as I have indicated elsewhere (Oliver, 1990), the limitations that our functional impairments impose upon us are an inadequate basis for building a political movement.

A second, related criticism contends that our subjective experiences of the 'pain' of both impairment and disability are ignored by the social model. Again, I find this censure partial and hard to countenance. If I simply focus on my own work, I co-wrote a book on male experiences of spinal cord injury (Oliver *et al.*, 1988) and undertook another study of the experiences of impairment, disability and ageing (Zarb and Oliver, 1993). More generally, I cannot accept assertions that the social model is not based upon disabled people's experiences. Quite the reverse, it emerged out of the experiences of disabled activists in the 1970s.

The third criticism of the social model states that it is unable to incorporate other social divisions, for example, 'race', gender, ageing, sexuality and so on. The fact that the social model has not so far adequately integrated these dimensions does not mean that it cannot ever do so. In my view it is not that the social model cannot cope with these issues but that analysts who wish to study these issues have not used it. Far better if the critics had spent less of their time criticizing the social model for its perceived failures and instead put more effort into attempting to apply it in practice to the areas of racism, sexism and sexuality.

A fourth criticism centres on the issue of 'otherness'. From this perspective, it is not the physical and environmental barriers that we face but the way our cultural values position disabled people as 'other'. This viewpoint is buttressed by recent developments in the theory of postmodernism and ideas about representation being crucial to disabled people. It is simply wrong to assert that, in principle, the social model ignores cultural values. More importantly, at the present time most disabled people in the world live in abject poverty, and do not have enough food and drink, while the two main causes of impairment internationally are war and poverty. As a consequence of this, any attempt to try to move disability politics exclusively into the realm of representation is fundamentally misguided and inappropriate when so many disabled people continue to experience life-threatening material deprivation.

The final criticism of the social model is that it is inadequate as a social theory of disablement. Now, the problem with this is that I do not think that those of us involved in the early discussions around the social model ever claimed that it was equivalent to a theory of disability. Indeed, most of us explicitly said these theoretical debates still needed to take place (Oliver, 1996b). And yet, an edited disability studies collection (Corker and French, 1998) spends a lot of time in the first and last chapters criticizing what are termed 'social model theorists' for their inadequacies before finally acknowledging that the social model is not a theory. It seems ridiculous to criticize the social model for not being something that it has never claimed to be.

These criticisms should not be seen merely as academic disputes, however heated and vitriolic they have become at times. They have also been part of the political terrain over which disability activists have

fought in the last ten years. There have been those who have been critical of the alleged formal or informal policing that has supposedly taken
place. For example, the journal *Disability and Society* has been accused
of only publishing articles on the social model that were ultimately
sympathetic to it. However, a count of articles published between the
first number in 2000 and the last number in 2002 demonstrates that the
journal published more than twenty papers which sought to criticize,
refine, review or even abandon the social model.

There is less dispute that some disability equality trainers, like some
racism awareness and sexism awareness trainers, have been over-zealous
in their promotion of the social model and have perhaps spent their
time trying to make non-disabled people feel guilty that they were
not disabled. However, that is clearly a problem with the application
of the model by some individuals rather than a flaw in the model
itself. Further, there is no doubt that the disabled people's movement
itself has sometimes been over-sensitive about its 'big idea', but that
has to be seen in the context of the way in which, throughout our
history, our ideas have been taken by others, used and indeed even
claimed for their own. This occurred in respect of the social model
when speaker after speaker from non-representative organizations for
disabled people claimed the social model as their own in the Trafalgar
Square demonstrations of 1994 in support of anti-discrimination legislation. Additionally, the now defunct Disability Rights Commission,
established in 1997 by the New Labour government, declared that it
was guided in everything it did by the social model of disability despite
often appearing not to understand what it was. More recently, many of
the big disability charities have claimed that the social model is central
to their own work.

This has led to some attempts to reclaim the social model, whatever
that means. My argument is that we do not have the time, the energy or
the resources to reclaim it, even if such a thing was possible. That would
reduce disability activism to the kind of intellectual masturbation in
which academics sometimes engage. Instead, we need to work out and
promote political strategies that are in line with the principles of the
social model. Never mind yet more talk about how we might reclaim
it, we need to get on and use it. We must not waste the gift that was
bestowed upon by those disability activists who were struggling against
the oppressive structures that kept disabled people out of society in the
1970s. For this reason for the remainder of this chapter I want to focus
on three areas or projects which I have been involved in over the last
twenty years that have sought to apply the social model, although I will

concentrate on a recent study of its implementation in Birmingham City Council.

The social model in action

The first project was my attempt to reconstruct social work with disabled people in accordance with the social model principles. It was intended to provide a counter to individualized casework that positioned disabled people as tragic victims in need of personalized therapeutic intervention. My book *Social Work with Disabled People* (Oliver, 1983) sought to switch social work intervention away from impaired individuals and target the disabling society. Moreover, the British Association of Social Workers (BASW) adopted it in 1986 as the way ahead for building a relationship between disabled people and social workers. In conjunction with BCODP, BASW organized a national conference to take it further, but after it nothing much happened and disability issues have remained a poor relation in equal opportunities social work training, and disabled people's needs have ranked very low down the agenda of most social service departments. There is little doubt that the hegemony of the individual model still endures within social work, as in other professions (Oliver and Sapey, 2006).

The social model then, has had no real impact on professional practice, and social work has failed to meet disabled people's self-articulated needs. Twenty years ago, I predicted that if social work was not prepared to change in terms of its practice relating to disabled people it would eventually disappear altogether (Oliver, 1983). Given the proposed changes by the Labour government in respect of modernizing social services, it seems likely that that forecast is about to come true. We can probably now announce the death of social work at least in relation to its involvement in the lives of disabled people.

A second illustration of the application of the social model was very evident in research on disability politics undertaken by Jane Campbell and myself. The social model of disability had become the 'big idea' of the disabled people's movement. A central reason for its impact was that it provided a shorthand way of linking up the many diverse experiences among people with a whole range of different impairments (Campbell and Oliver, 1996). Prior to the late 1970s and early 1980s disabled people's attempts at self-organization had always floundered on the conflicts between the specific impairments and the different experiences of disablement that they generated.

The social model was a way of getting us all to think about the things we had in common, and the barriers that we all faced. Of course, some of those barriers were impairment-specific; for example, blind people might have information barriers, people with mobility restrictions might have access barriers, deaf people communication barriers and so on. Nevertheless, the social model became a way in which to link up all of those kinds of experiences and enabled the movement to develop a collective consciousness that enabled it to expand at a rapid rate throughout the 1980s.

Yet, in the 1990s, independent living and disabled people's rights emerged as key ideas to sit alongside the social model. This, coupled with the increasing disputes about the meaning of the social model, has led some activists, notably Vic Finkelstein, to claim that the movement has lost its way and needs to return to its roots. What is clear is that as we move into the twenty-first century, the social model of disability is no longer the glue that binds the movement together in the way that it did in the 1980s. Instead, it has been relegated to the back burner, and its radical potential has been put on hold while the disability leadership has become involved in parliamentary campaigns to improve disabled people's rights and to enhance the services necessary to support 'independent living'.

The third social model project that I want to discuss was carried out with Birmingham City Council (Oliver and Bailey, 2002). While many local authorities (and indeed other agencies) have signed up to the social model, none has successfully implemented it as the means to providing services to disabled people. There are no blueprints to guide its implementation and there is not a substantial body of experience on how to do it. This is not necessarily a bad thing, however, because the social model is nothing more than a practical tool to facilitate the restructuring of services and hence can be adapted to specific local contexts, needs and circumstances.

In 1996, Birmingham City Council adopted the social model as a guide to service provision for disabled people. However, like many organizations that claim to endorse the social model, when it was reviewed five years later nothing much had happened. In 2001, I was commissioned to provide a report suggesting ways in which the City Council could take forward its renewed commitment to the social model. I worked with a disabled colleague, Peter Bailey, and conducted a wide range of visits, meetings and consultations. We concluded that, in Birmingham, the influence of the social model of disability varied greatly, with evidence of its impact in some areas, but in many others it was perceived as largely irrelevant, if not flawed. In discussions, it was possible to identify three broad approaches to service provision among providers there, which we termed humanitarian, compliance and citizenship.

The humanitarian approach

In this perspective, services were provided out of goodwill and the desire to help individuals and groups perceived as less fortunate. This meant that a medical approach was all pervasive, with the professional experts in control of service provision, while the disabled person was regarded as 'the problem'. Hence, users were expected to be grateful for receiving these services. A characteristic outcome was that producers thought they were doing a good job even though users, when asked, were often critical. As a result, the relationship between service providers and disabled users was characterized by conflict, with a lack of trust, and dissatisfaction with existing services because they were unreliable and inadequate. In Birmingham, as elsewhere, disabled people do not like being patronized or not valued as human beings.

As an illustration, the Ring and Ride service had been set up as a way of compensating disabled people for the lack of accessible transport. Thus, the Council funded an alternative service, but control remained firmly with the provider. What was available fell far short of meeting disabled people's needs, and many complained that the service had been set up for second-class citizens, which they felt powerless to change. Another example of the humanitarian approach existed in the provision of residential care places. This was usually arranged out of a genuine desire to help disabled people, but with staff again in effective control, disabled users feared that the residential 'solution' would be long term. With little autonomy in how they led their lives, disabled inmates were at risk of becoming institutionalized, and invariably ended up with a poorer quality of life than they had the right to expect.

The compliance approach

From the 'compliance' perspective, government policy and legislation drive service provision. Obviously the Disability Discrimination Act (DDA) (1995) is of prime importance in respect of services to disabled people but other legislation such as the NHS and Community Care Act (1990) and even the Chronically Sick and Disabled Act (1970) are also relevant. Despite the stated objectives of such initiatives, producers have typically seen their role as doing the minimum amount required complying with the law or government regulations. Needless to say, service users in Birmingham often felt disgruntled because they did not think that services were being organized according to disabled people's support needs or rights. It was the producers who interpreted the laws, rules and regulations, often adopting a checklist, or task-oriented approach, that simply satisfied basic standards and demonstrated little sense of commitment to wider service goals or to a partnership with disabled users. As a result, the compliance approach was characterized by conflict, a denial of entitlements and expectations, inadequate services and low levels of user satisfaction.

An illustration of the compliance approach was provided in the home care or home support service, where disabled people should have received personal support to maintain an appropriate degree of control, independence and autonomy in their own homes. In practice, staff provided a service to help disabled users go to bed at the end of the day, yet they had to fit in with when staff were available to provide such support. As a consequence, the service did not meet many users' needs, but they dared not complain for fear of damaging important relationships. Conversely, the providers were so focused on their problems that they found it hard to see users as equals, or align themselves with the aim of user empowerment.

The citizenship approach

In this approach, disabled people were regarded as equal citizens with full rights and responsibilities. Three main dimensions were identified:

(a) Economic: disabled people were seen as contributing members of society as both workers and valued customers or users.
(b) Political: disabled people were recognized as empowered individuals, voters and a powerful interest group.
(c) Moral: disabled people were seen as active citizens with all that implies in terms of rights and responsibilities.

Only when all three dimensions are met will the relationship between providers and users of services be a truly harmonious one and we found few examples in Birmingham.

One example of the citizenship approach was evident in the direct payments system. It stressed the following points:

• the user makes direct payments to the person of their choice to provide personal support;

- the support worker identifies the disabled person as the person with the power to end the relationship and the income source;
- the support worker identifies with the overall aims of the relationship, not specific tasks, like getting someone to bed;
- the user expects the support worker to turn up on time and therefore can take on work and other commitments;
- the user makes the decisions about how they want to treated by support staff.

This citizenship approach contrasted with traditional practices such as giving discounts to disabled people for some council services, including leisure services like swimming. The basis on which a discount was applied was often lost in history and continued simply because disabled people are relatively poorer as a group. However, this is the application of a stereotype unthinkable in a 'race' or gender context. An alternative rationale might be that full access to the service is not available to some disabled people. However, this sustained the compensatory culture that has for so long undermined disabled people's struggle for equality in Birmingham and elsewhere. Such compensation is not consistent with the social model or a citizenship approach. What disabled people are seeking is as end to social oppression and discrimination, not compensation for their continued exclusion.

We concluded that services for disabled people in Birmingham overall were still largely provided under the humanitarian and compliance approaches. However, the Council was moving towards a citizenship approach in terms of services to its ethnic minorities and we suggested that there was no reason why it could not do the same in respect of disabled people.

Implementing a citizenship approach

Departmental services in Birmingham had no single driver, and the formal corporate commitment to the social model in 1995 was widely ignored. The Disability Discrimination Act (1995) was having some effect on services but the compliance was mostly fairly limited and partial. It was evident that, beyond a generalized commitment to the humanitarian approach, few elected members showed any real commitment to disability issues.

Nationally, we know that the main disability charities that drove the humanitarian-based disability agenda for so many years had limited aspirations for disabled people. These could be summed up as a need for good medical care, a comfortable place to live and to be protected from those that might take advantage of them. More recently the welfare agenda has been driven by professionals, both within charities and the voluntary sector and within the state, and has moved towards a compliance approach. This contrasts starkly with disabled people's agenda, which focuses on issues such as employment and social inclusion, independent living and civil rights.

Recently the government has made it clear that its idea of citizenship encompasses rights and entitlements as well as duties and responsibilities. Thus, disabled people should be given fair and equal opportunities to compete in the labour market. Despite a number of important and innovative initiatives aimed at getting disabled people into the workforce, only 0.8 per cent of the Birmingham City Council workforce is disabled. In contrast, the Council has set a target of 20 per cent for people from ethnic minority communities. We suggested that adopting a firm target and formulating appropriate plans for the employment of disabled people would have a positive impact and help to overcome the poor response rate among disabled people when jobs are advertised. Finally, we suggested that it was important that those disabled employees already in post to be afforded opportunities for promotion and advancement equal to that of the rest of the population. This further presumes that disabled people can secure an education and training that provides them with the necessary qualifications and skills.

Of course, other factors like race, gender, age and sexuality also have a considerable impact on how disability is experienced. We found little evidence to suggest that service providers or planners in Birmingham were aware of, or sensitive to, the need to recognize such diversity. Again, the only way to ensure that services do not institutionally discriminate against minority groups of disabled people is to consult widely about their needs. While Council departments assured us that they consulted regularly with users and in a meaningful way, disabled people often told a different story. Some felt that consultation was tokenistic and even where there were well-established user groups, only 'the chosen few' were consulted and this usually resulted in the department concerned implementing policies that it had already decided on.

The social model is incompatible with taking an impairment-specific approach to disabled people. However, we did make an exception in the case of deaf people in Birmingham, many of whom do not see themselves as part of a disabled community but as a linguistic minority. This is in line with the way deaf people nationally see themselves and there is considerable pressure on government to recognize British Sign Language as a language in its own right. That said, the social model of disability recognizes that the communication problems faced by deaf people are not because they are unable to speak but because the rest of us do not speak their language.

There is little point in asking whether the social model was an adequate framework for revamping disability services in Birmingham or whether we accurately translated the principles of the social model as recommendations for action. The real test will be in five or ten or fifteen years, when it should be possible to determine its impact in improving the lives of disabled people in Birmingham.

Conclusion

Throughout this chapter I have argued that the social model of disability is a practical tool like a hammer or a screwdriver, not a theory, an idea or a concept. Furthermore, I have suggested that too much time has been spent discussing it rather than attempting to use it as a tool to produce social and political change. If we imagine that throughout human history the carpenters and builders of the world had spent their time talking about whether the hammer or screwdriver were adequate tools for the purpose of building houses, we would still be living in caves or roaming the plains. However, we do have a hammer in the disabled people's movement and, if properly used, the social model of disability could become the means of achieving justice and freedom for disabled people 'all over this land'.

4

Unmet Promises of Disability Law and Policy

There are three reasons for deciding to include this piece in the new edition. To begin with it shows how, even in two of the richest countries in the world with their own disability discrimination legislation, the reality of public exclusion still remains. Additionally, it shows how personal experiences can become the basis for sociological analysis and, finally, it enables me to express my anger and frustration at no longer flying because of my experiences described herein. It explores my own and a blind colleague's experiences of using public transport systems in our respective countries of residence and their failures to take account of our needs. It then analyzes the implications for law and policy and suggests that transport systems have a long way to go before they adequately meet the needs of disabled travellers. It was co-written with an American colleague Beth Omansky and originally published in an American social studies reader (Rosenblum and Travis, 2003).

Beth and I, among many academics from all over the world, were invited to a prestigious international conference in Washington, DC in 2000 and our attempts to get there and socialize at the event are described below. I have not flown since on either business or pleasure and I bitterly resent the fact that my life is less rewarding and exciting than it should be. I still get extremely angry when we are told by travel agents and airlines that the problems of travelling as a severely impaired person have now been resolved. I still become incandescent with rage when we are told by governments and disability organizations that voluntary codes of practice are the way ahead.

The reality is that most transport providers, whether public agencies or private companies, are now too big and powerful for cowardly governments to take them on. Even where enforcement mechanisms exist they are often not properly policed and enforced. For example, while our local authorities are supposed to ensure the access of local taxi fleets, I still find it impossible to go out for a drink with my mates on a Friday night or my family for Sunday lunch because there is no guarantee that I will be able to get home even if I can get there. Ironically, if I wanted to go to the day centre or supermarket on a weekday, I would have plenty of taxis vying for my custom. My local authority is simply not willing to take on the assembled might of local taxi drivers.

While this is obviously a personal gripe, it does say something about our society. In Britain we have been taught since our child-hoods that not having a formal contract between state and citizen that specifies the rights and responsibilities of both in a written con-stitution contributes to the strength of our democracy. In fact, it does nothing of the sort; it enables greedy politicians, ambitious policy-makers and ineffective professionals to pursue their own careers at the expense of the ordinary citizen. If this is not the case, then surely politicians can produce a written constitution that guarantees us our rights and that ensures that we meet our responsibilities and pass legislation that effectively guarantees that this balance can be ensured. We will then have a democratic system that is truly fit for twenty-first-century purpose, but don't hold your breath.

~~~~~~~~~~

How long must we wait? Unmet promises of disability law and policy

(written by Mike Oliver and Beth Omansky)

All we really want to do

In the autumn of 2000 we were invited to attend a prestigious inter-national conference in Washington, DC to launch the discipline of disability studies onto the academic world. We eagerly accepted the invitation and looked forward to a stimulating few days in interaction with academic colleagues from around the globe. This is a scenario not unknown to many thousands of international academics. However, we would argue, our experiences as disabled academics set us apart from those of our non-disabled colleagues because of the discriminatory treatment we face in doing ordinary things that our non-disabled colleagues take for granted; in this case, using the transport system.

Before going on to document the discriminatory treatment we both faced, there are a number of preliminary points we wish to make. To begin with, we recognize that using public transportation can be a difficult experience for all concerned, but we wish to exert that our experiences as disabled travellers go far beyond what the non-disabled traveller has to endure. Additionally, when millions of disabled people all over the world still have their basic human rights denied to them, we feel uneasy about highlighting the personal difficulties of a few relatively privileged ones from the minority world.

Finally, as academics working in a discipline where personal experience is seen as pivotal to our understanding of the world and the ways it operates, we make no apologies for describing our own discriminatory and degrading treatment though we will try to use these personal experiences as a framework for broader analysis. In so doing, initially I will describe my experiences of flying to Washington, DC for the conference and then Beth will discuss her attempts to use the local transportation system to socialize with academic colleagues. We will then end by considering some of the general issues raised.

Leaving on a jet plane

(written by Mike Oliver)

When I received an invitation to attend the conference in Washington, DC I was unsure whether or not to accept because it would mean that I would have to fly from Britain to the USA and I have had many unpleasant travel experiences in the past. I have been ignored, abused, patronized, dropped on the floor and often handled worse than the dead meat that is served to the passengers on the flight, all because I use an electric wheelchair and require manual assistance. It seems incredible that when we have the technology to send people into space we still find it difficult to enable disabled people to get on and off aeroplanes with their dignity and self-respect still intact. However, I decided that the promise of the conference, plus the opportunity to socialize with other academics with interests similar to mine, was too good to miss.

The first hassle, I knew from experience, would be in trying to find an airline that would permit me to pre-book seats that would give me enough leg room to enable me to sit comfortably and safely. 'It's not allowed'; 'IATA regulations don't permit it'; 'It's up to the Captain'; 'We don't know how the plane will be loaded'; 'You're not allowed to block exits'; 'We don't know what plane we will be using' are all excuses I have been given in the past. After several angry phone calls and an exchange of letters, I am eventually allowed to book seats which will give me the leg room I require and I know that the first battle is over.

The next hassle comes when I check in at Heathrow, London, one of the world's busiest airports. On arrival at check-in, the staff insist that I transfer out of my electric wheelchair and into one of their manual ones. I explain that that will mean me sitting in an uncomfortable chair for at least three hours as well as restricting my personal mobility. The equivalent for a non-disabled traveller would be the enforced wearing of someone else's shoes while being denied access to refreshments, duty free shopping and so on. My request that I be allowed to remain in my own wheelchair until I board the plane is turned down on health and safety grounds. I politely enquire as to what the rules are and am told that the ground crew will not lift my wheelchair down the stairs from the gate to the tarmac for stowing in the hold.

Reluctantly I agree to get out of my chair and I prepare myself for the next hassle. After a few minutes wait, two men turn up with a manual wheelchair and proceed to lift me bodily into it, in full view of those queuing for the flight as well as anyone else who wants to watch. This was managed reasonably competently but I feel that it is hardly appropriate treatment for anyone to endure. It gets worse, however, because the two men then try to dismantle my electric wheelchair and disconnect the batteries. I explain to them that the chair does not dismantle and the batteries are dry cell and do not need to be disconnected. They tell me that they must disconnect the batteries and I insist that it is unnecessary.

At this point my wife, Joy, who is travelling with me as my personal assistant, intervenes and calls the supervisor. After a heated argument and several phone calls, it is agreed that dry cell batteries do not need to be disconnected and the men and my wheelchair disappear into the bowels of the airport. As I watch it go, there is no guarantee that they, or the ground crew who will lift it into the hold, will not disconnect the batteries or indeed, remove them altogether. The experience of a friend of mine briefly comes to mind. She flew from Heathrow recently, only to notice that her chair was still on the ground as the plane took off. Not only had they refused to load it but they had also neglected to tell her. Still we were now checked in so I prepare myself for the next battle.

This comes some two hours later when I am taken to the gate for boarding. I am told that I would be loaded before the rest of the passengers, which would at least preserve my privacy, if not my dignity. Unfortunately, however, the two men designated to carry me on to the plane are late and only arrive as other passengers are being boarded. This means a further delay until I am taken onto the jetty and down to the door of the aircraft. On reaching this point, a small lifting chair is produced and I am transferred from the airport wheelchair onto it. It is wholly unsuitable because it has no arms and does not take into account the fact that I have no balance. Eventually I am strapped to it and carried onto the aircraft, which is now full.

I am carried past row after row of passengers until I reach my seat. I am then lifted bodily into the aircraft seat but there are a number of problems with this. The space is very confined and does not give the lifters much room and the arms of the aircraft seat are not detachable. As a consequence of this I am virtually dragged over the arm. What physical damage this is causing I don't know as I have no sensation in that part of my body but the dragging does pull my trousers down and exposes large amounts of naked flesh to the rest of the passengers. Eventually I am placed in the seat and my wife helps me to rearrange my clothing more appropriately.

I now settle down for the nine-hour flight but realize that I must moderate my food and liquid intake, for it is impossible for me to get to the toilet on the aircraft. We arrive in the Washington, DC suburbs. The rest of the passengers are disembarked onto 'mobile lounges'; Dulles International Airport does not have jetties. We are to be put on the last one with the remaining passengers but unfortunately, while this lounge does have a chair to carry me off in, there are no personnel to lift me. A row then breaks out between airport staff and cabin crew as to whose responsibility it is to get me off the aircraft. This causes delays and clearly angers a tired cabin crew who want, quite rightly, to get off the aircraft themselves and end their shift.

The situation is eventually resolved when a member of the cabin crew and the flight engineer agree to lift me off the aircraft. This they do but they are not trained so to do and once again I am dragged across the aircraft seat arm and my clothing again comes adrift. I am placed onto the mobile lounge but another row breaks out as I must now be transferred into one of the fixed seats. Again, this is eventually done but with no consideration for my dignity and privacy and some threat to my health status as I feel that I am being thrown about by untrained and angry people.

The mobile lounge then does its job and takes us back to the terminal building where I expect my old, familiar and safe wheelchair to be waiting. It is not. I am informed that I must now transfer into one of the airport wheelchairs before proceeding to the collection point for our suitcases and my wheelchair. There are two problems with this: their wheelchair does not have detachable arms and there is no one to lift me. Another row breaks out and eventually two airport staff volunteer to lift me into the airport's chair. Again, this is managed with great difficulty and some danger to all of us as they are willing but untrained.

Eventually I am reunited with my own chair and I begin to relax. I decide to complain formally and demand to see someone in charge. A supervisor appears and informs me that getting on and off the aircraft is my responsibility and that I should have been lifted off by my wife and two colleagues who are travelling with us, one of whom is himself disabled and the other has a history of chronic back problems. At this point I leave as I desperately need a drink and to get to the hotel to survey any damage that may have been inflicted. Once I am in bed I find that I have severe lacerations and bruising to my buttocks. It takes me several hours before I am able to stop shaking. Still, I am here and I look forward to the next four days, though in the back of my mind I know I have to go through it all again in order to get home.

Everything is broken

(written by Beth Omansky)

Knowing that my British colleagues have a predilection for American blues music, I make reservations at a supper club where we will meet. I first met Mike and his colleague, Len, briefly at a conference in Chicago earlier in the year, and I found much in common with them. I am excited at the prospect of spending Sunday evening socializing and exchanging ideas with internationally renowned scholars on the first night of their visit to Washington, DC.

Mike calls my home at about three o'clock on the Sunday afternoon of their arrival to say they are finally settled in at the hotel. He sounds perturbed, apparently due to mistreatment by airport employees at Dulles Airport, but still wishes to get together. I give him the name and address of the blues club, and we decide to meet at seven o'clock that evening. Mike will contact the DC taxicab company to arrange for a wheelchair-accessible van.

About half an hour later, Mike calls back with our first piece of bad news: there is no wheelchair-accessible taxicab service to travel from one location to another within the District of Columbia. Absurdly enough, while you can go from DC into the Virginia or Maryland suburbs and back into DC, the taxi service will not take you between locations within the District. I am astonished and baffled by the logic of this policy. I wonder if this is just a means to charge more by forcing disabled people to take lengthy detours into the suburbs and back again, or to discourage them from riding taxis altogether. We forgo any plan to find another music club that is both wheelchair and distance accessible, and choose instead to find a restaurant near the hotel where Mike, Joy and Len are staying.

I plan to take the nine-mile ride from my home into the District via MetroAccess, the DC metropolitan area's paratransit system for disabled people. The Americans With Disabilities Act of 1990 (ADA) is a civil rights law designed to prohibit discrimination and to ensure equal access to transportation, employment, public accommodations, public services and telecommunications. The law mandates paratransit services, usually comprised of a fleet of wheelchair-accessible vans and perhaps some cars. The Washington Metropolitan Area Transit Authority (WMATA) sponsors MetroAccess paratransit service, but subcontracts the work out to local governments and other local fixed-route transit systems, including privately owned for-profit companies in the metropolitan area.

Being considered disabled under the ADA is not enough to be considered eligible for paratransit ridership; disabled people must go through a certification process. Applicants must complete a lengthy, two-part form, Part A to be filled out by the applicant, Part B to be completed by a physician. Eligibility is based on a person's 'functional limitation', assessed by an occupational therapist or other medical professional that is determined (and paid) by MetroAccess officials to be qualified to judge each applicant's ability to ride public fixed-route transit. In the main, able-bodied medical professionals determine who is eligible and who is denied access to paratransit. They are gatekeepers who lack personal expertise about what it is like to be disabled by an inaccessible environment. Applicants are judged on their ability to walk or travel up to a quarter of a mile, travel independently to and from bus stops, identify the correct bus or bus stop to board or get off, get on or off a bus or train using a lift, and ask for and understand instructions to board, ride and disembark. Disabled people often encounter a well-crafted double-bind in the assessment process: if assessors determine that applicants' 'mobility skills' are adequate, they are deemed able to ride public fixed-route transit, and thus declared ineligible for MetroAccess. But, if assessors decide that applicants lack good mobility skills, they may be denied MetroAccess services and told to get additional mobility training.

The ADA's promise of equal transportation access for disabled people has thus far failed to meet even minimal expectations. Like hundreds of other disabled workers, I rely on MetroAccess to take me to and from work. I rely on it to get me to school at least twice a week, to out-of-office work-related appointments, to medical appointments and to social engagements. MetroAccess has caused me to be more than an hour late for work appointments, school and doctor's appointments more times than I can count and I have missed some of these obligations altogether when my rides failed to show up at all. During my first semester in school, MetroAccess failed to pick me up after class even one time and I was left stranded in DC, at ten-thirty at night, in freezing cold weather, with locked school buildings all around me and with no way home. On four separate occasions, MetroAccess failed to pick me up for rides to the airport, forcing me to spend $40 on taxicabs for what should have been $2.20 on the van.

Scheduling is notoriously bad. Drivers are frustrated by the impossible situation of rides that are scheduled too close together and they often have no time for breaks during what can be twelve-hour shifts. Exhausted, frazzled drivers cannot help but be hazardous drivers.

Routing has little or no logic. Passengers are forced to share rides that take them in opposite directions than intended. Because MetroAccess is a ride-share service, its policy states that passengers are not supposed to be on the van for twenty minutes longer than it would normally take for them to go from one particular destination to another. This ostensibly saves people from having to ride all over the DC Metro area, picking up and dropping off other clients. Once, I rode on the van around the District for exactly one hour, for what should have been a twenty-minute ride had we taken a direct route. At the end of that hour, I looked out the window and saw the exact location where I had been picked up. I had been driven around in one big circle, no closer to home than I was before I boarded the van. Another time, I watched as the van drove right past the freeway exit to my home to drop off another client who lived ten miles down the road. Because of this, I rode an extra twenty miles unnecessarily.

The next time a van came to take me to school, I asked the driver, 'Am I ride-sharing today? How long will I be on the van?' He checked his manifest, and then said, 'Yes, you are ride-sharing, so you will probably be on the van about an hour and a half.' I said, 'I can't do that

today. I just don't have the time. Please let me off the van.' He refused
to open the door. He said, 'You are already on the van. You must stay
on the van until we reach your destination. Go sit down and buckle
your seat belt.' I said, 'We are still at my house. The van is not moving.
Let me off.' Again he refused and ordered me to sit down. I refused.
He radioed the dispatch office to find out what he should do with
me. The dispatcher said he would have to check with a supervisor.
The minutes ticked by. Finally, after ten minutes, they agreed to let
me off the van. Other times, when I protested circuitous routing and
unjustifiable amounts of time riding around, drivers scolded me, saying
such things as, 'Just sit there and be quiet. Your ride costs only $2.20,
so you should be grateful for it.' Drivers, dispatchers and supervisors
have rebuked me in this manner enough times to have me believe that
their attitudes are a reflection of WMATA culture. MetroAccess is not
a charity-based service. I am a taxpayer who contributes to the system,
including to its employee salaries. Sometimes, I feel that they treat me
as if I were a sack of groceries, as something less than human.

My experiences with MetroAccess are not unique. When I ride-
share with other disabled people, we often swap MetroAccess horror
stories, establishing a pattern of abuses. At least five times that I know
of, local television stations have run investigative pieces, providing
video and audio documentation of how disabled people are treated by
MetroAccess. One reporter filmed a faulty lift, with a wheelchair user
in mid-air while the driver banged on the apparatus with a crowbar in
a futile effort to force the lift to function. Once, I was on a van from
DC to my home when the driver told me that he had to be careful
which route he took because his reverse gear was broken and he had
to route himself to avoid having to back up. Seat belts are often not in
working order and the ride in the back of the vans is so bumpy that
your voice shakes when you try to talk.

Everyone interviewed had similar stories of being picked up hours
late or not at all. A young woman reported that MetroAccess caused
her to be very late to an interview for her first job. She did not get the
job. Ironically, many times clients who have cancelled their rides in
advance have found that the vans showed up at their doors anyway. This
does not matter to MetroAccess subcontractors because they are paid
per trip, whether or not clients actually ride. On top of that, clients
are penalized for this practice because they are listed as 'no-shows',
which goes against them on their MetroAccess records. Since so many
MetroAccess riders have noted this practice, I wonder if cancelled rides
are left on manifests on purpose.

Clients report spending up to half an hour on hold waiting for the dispatch office to answer phone enquiries about where their rides are. Many times, while they are inside a building, on hold for the dispatcher, the vans have come and gone without the riders knowing. Dispatchers refuse to send the van back because it is already on its way to the next destination. Dialysis patients have reported being dropped off at dialysis centres and then abandoned even though their return ride home had been confirmed earlier. Wheelchair users report that their chairs were strapped down incorrectly, causing them to slide around dangerously in the back of the van. In one of the television reports, the chief executive officer of WMATA responded with a note of surprise, as if he had never heard the complaints before. He said in a voice choked with mock sorrow, 'We will do better.' But the years go by and nothing changes.

Because I have had my booking either fall off or omitted from manifests so often in the past, I have learned to check and recheck with the scheduling office to make sure my ride is still listed. Nevertheless, this is no guarantee that the driver will arrive on time, or at all for that matter. Therefore, I made sure to call the reservation and dispatch centre earlier in the day to confirm that I was, indeed, on the manifest for a six o'clock pick-up to travel into DC to meet Mike, Joy and Len, then to go back home four hours later. Now it's six o'clock and the van is not here. Tension vaguely gnaws at the back of my neck, causing the muscles to stiffen and ache. I know that MetroAccess allows itself a fifteen-minute window on either side of my pick-up time, so I wait until six-fifteen before I call the office. The dispatcher reassures me that the van is scheduled to pick me up at 6pm and that it should be there any moment. I ask her to check with the driver for his estimated time of arrival. She responds curtly, 'I told you it will be there any minute', and disconnects the call before I can reply. I wait some more.

By six-thirty my anxiety has given way to frustration. I call the dispatch office again. A man answers. I say, 'My ride was supposed to be here a half an hour ago. Would you please radio the driver?' After placing me on hold for approximately ten minutes, he tells me, 'I think we have a mix-up. I'll call you back in a few minutes.' Twenty minutes later he calls to say, 'We booked you on Fastran (one of the local government's services), but Fastran doesn't run on weekends.' I have never ceased to be amazed at the creativity of MetroAccess's blunders, but this one takes the cake.

I know that by now my colleagues are expecting me to meet them at the hotel bar. I call their room repeatedly and leave messages.

I call the hotel to have them paged at the bar, but there is no paging system there. There is nothing I can do but wait to hear from them. Upset and disappointed, I resign myself to the fact that MetroAccess has spoiled my plans. I will not have my long-awaited, well-planned evening with my British colleagues. Once again, I have been disabled by MetroAccess system failures.

May the light shine on the truth someday

(written by Mike Oliver and Beth Omansky)

We have recounted our own personal experiences of interactions with global and local transport systems and we feel crushed by them. We can (and do) complain vociferously, campaign for the law to be changed, demonstrate on the streets, take our stories to the media and so on, but complaints are easily managed by large organizations. Laws take a long time to change and while taking to the streets is personally empowering, it will not enable us to go to the next conference, let alone socialize together when we are there.

There are things we need to understand from these crushing experiences. To begin with, it is testament to the global power of the airlines that, even though there is civil rights legislation in both Britain and America, air travel is exempt from those laws. This is hardly surprising for an industry that pays almost no tax on the fuel it uses and that persuades governments to compensate it for an industry recession it created itself via over-pricing and poor service to customers. Clearly, the airline industry pays little or no attention to the needs of disabled travellers. As each new generation of aircraft comes off the drawing board, we continue to be designed out, rather than included in. With regard to ground transportation, government subcontracting of public services to for-profit companies dramatically shifts priorities away from democratic principles of inclusion, and towards the bottom line of profit margins instead.

It is a fact that American civil rights legislation is the most comprehensive and enforceable in the world. Still it fails to ensure that disabled American citizens and their guests can move around their communities when and how they choose. This failure suggests that such legislation promises much more than it delivers. Indeed, we even begin to wonder whether such legislation is nothing more than a confidence trick, actually protecting the interests of the rich and powerful rather than ensuring that the rights of all citizens are actually being properly addressed.

Finally, and most importantly, we would like to return to a point we made earlier. If these are the kinds of everyday experience that we, as relatively privileged and empowered disabled people, have to endure, what is life really like for those millions of underprivileged and disempowered disabled people who exist in all parts of the world? In talking about our own personal experiences, we hope we have shone some light on the truth of just how far we have to go in order to build a world that fully includes all disabled people.

5

Special Education into the Twenty-first Century

Education is something we all have experienced, either as teachers or learners; some of us have been both. As I have already indicated, my experiences at school were not particularly happy ones. When I found myself on the giving rather than receiving end of what we call teaching, my initial approach was to copy the way I had been taught. Why I did this I'm not sure because that approach had alienated me from the education system. Fortunately, I quickly came to realize that there were better ways and I found myself adopting what I would now call a 'social model' approach to teaching long before I had ever thought of the term 'social model'. With the help of a supportive mentor I soon learned that the 'art' of teaching was to create the right conditions for people to learn for themselves.

Looking back on my career as a provider of educational resources (I am more comfortable with this term than teacher), I am now convinced that I have never taught anyone anything but I hope I have created the right conditions and environments for people to learn things for themselves. In this enterprise I hope I have been successful and, for all those hard-pressed teachers out there forced to deliver the national curriculum or else, I do realize that I have been fortunate to work in establishments conducive to and with colleagues supportive of this approach. I mention it here to indicate that I was a 'social modellist' even before I knew what the social model was.

There are a number of reasons for including this chapter in the book. It attempts to combine some of my own personal experiences when I worked as a special education lecturer with attempts to theorize about the changes that were occurring as the millennium approached. It also attempts to consider the implications of these changes, not just for the development of special needs education but education in general. It was originally given as a keynote address at the International Special Education Conference, Manchester, 'Including the Excluded', in 2000. However, I have made some changes to the original paper for this book for reasons that I outline below.

At this juncture it would be dishonest not to admit that many of the changes that social theorists, myself included, envisaged have not occurred or have not occurred in the way that we thought they might. In fact, the first few years of the new millennium have shown just how resistant our educational, economic and social systems have been to change, in the short term at least. I still believe that the future for special education is bleak but it is not going to disappear for a long time to come. I also need to admit that, when I came back to this paper after several years, I was surprised that much of the terminology used was academically pretentious. So I have changed some of the language and terminology in order to clarify my argument. I have resisted the temptation to change the title, however, in order to demonstrate how pretentious academics can be sometimes.

~~~~~~~~~~

Decoupling education policy from the economy in late capitalist societies: some implications for special education

Introduction

A few years ago in a keynote address I gave to the Irish Association of Teachers in Special Education (IATSE) I posed the question, does special education have a role to play in the twenty-first century? I came to the conclusion that it did not and that 'nothing short of a radical deconstruction of special education and the reconstruction of education in totality will be enough – even if it takes us another hundred years' (Oliver, 1995, p. 67).

While I have tried to specify some of the changes necessary for this reconstruction to take place (see Oliver, 1996b, Chapter 6), in this paper I want to take this further and suggest that at this point in our history fundamental changes are occurring in our lives and our worlds and that these will have profound implications for education in general, as well as for special education in particular. In order to begin to grasp the magnitude of all this, I will need to examine recent attempts to theorize what some writers have called the end of modernity. Thus, I will locate my arguments within debates about the coming of what has variously been called postmodernity (Bauman, 1992), high modernity (Giddens, 1990) or late capitalism (Jameson, 1991).

It would not be untrue to say that, while these debates have raged within social theory for some time now, by and large they have passed by attempts to theorize special education (see for example Clark, Dyson and Millward, 1998). Hence, as one educationalist has pointed out:

> The symbiotic relationship between regular and special education constrains theory making. Special educational theorising will not of itself challenge its central cannons to effect a reconstruction of schooling. The challenge has to be imported. (Slee, 1998, p. 136)

In attempting to rise to this challenge and to import social theorizing into special education, there are a number of preliminary points that I need to make. Most social theorists agree that we are entering a period of profound change for the societies in which we live, although different theorists use different terminology to refer to these changes. The nature and scope of these changes will be discussed further later in the chapter. We have also seen changes to the nature of theorizing itself. The goal of objectivity has broken down in the face of criticisms from a variety of disempowered and disenfranchised groups (Clough and Barton, 1999) to the point where personal experience has sometimes become a standpoint epistemology. The overall outcome of this has been that theorists have begun to doubt themselves and disempowered and disenfranchised groups have accused theory of being either unrepresentative of or irrelevant to the lives of most people. The solution to this dilemma, according to Carol Thomas (1999), is to combine structural analysis with writing oneself into the picture.

Accordingly, in the first part of this paper I will describe my own intellectual journey, which led me to believe that there is no place for special education in the world to which we are moving. In the second and third parts, I will attempt to add a structural analysis to this by looking at some of the economic and social forces which are beginning to sound the death knell for special education, whatever it does and however it tries to reconstruct itself. Finally, I will look at the future by writing myself back into the picture and suggesting that an active engagement in the politics of the real world can contribute to building a more inclusive world.

The special education paradigm: a personal account

My critique of special education and subsequent calls for its abolition have not been based upon direct personal experience. I never attended a special school as a pupil, though many of my friends did and I have heard them talk bitterly about their experiences. My own experience came initially when I taught, or more accurately attempted to teach, young offenders to read and write and subsequently when, as a lecturer in special educational needs, I visited numerous special and ordinary schools that were attempting to meet the special educational needs of their children. Finally, I served as a member of the Fish Committee, which reviewed special needs provision in Inner London in the 1980s. During this time I met many committed and dedicated professionals and many contented children.

I make these points in order to separate out my attitude to and experience of special education. While my experiences, in many instances were positive, I was and remain implacably opposed to the very existence of special education. This attitude was shaped crucially by a document called the *Fundamental Principles of Disability* (UPIAS, 1976), produced by an organization of disabled people known as the Union of the Physically Impaired Against Segregation. This document not only called for the abolition of all institutions that segregated disabled people but provided a rationale and justification for so doing. All my subsequent work, including that on education, has been shaped by this 'little red book' (Oliver, 1996b). The point I am trying to make here is that my critique of special education has been a conceptual, analytical and political one and not one deriving from some unfortunate personal experiences in special schools.

In describing my thinking about special education, I propose to make use of the work of Thomas Kuhn (1970) on 'knowledge paradigms'. In his great work *The Structure of Scientific Revolutions* he describes how knowledge paradigms replace one another, not through the gradual evolution of our understanding and the accumulation of facts about the world but through the emergence of what he called anomalies in the existing paradigm. Eventually, he argues, these anomalies become so great that they force a shift to an entirely new paradigm through nothing more or less than a complete revolution in our thinking.

This idea of the replacement of one paradigm by another through a knowledge revolution is helpful in understanding our current experience in special education; in Kuhn's terms, we are moving from a special to an inclusive education paradigm. In my view, the anomalies in the special education paradigm are becoming so numerous that we are approaching 'paradigm incommensurability', by which Kuhn meant that the particular worldview was falling apart and was becoming unsustainable (*ibid.*). In discussing the emergence of anomalies in the special education paradigm I shall first discuss those personal anomalies that resulted from my own direct experience before going on to discuss anomalies that have emerged through developments in policy and practice.

I met a young man whom I shall call 'Foxy' thirty years ago when I attempted to teach him in the young offenders' prison where I then worked. He had been labelled as educationally subnormal (severe) and his IQ was recorded as fifty-five. Despite his attempts and mine he couldn't read a word on the day I met him and he still couldn't read a word on the day he was discharged from the prison some eighteen months later. Foxy was a passionate fan of Southampton Football Club and he claimed to know not only the result of every match they had played since the end of the Second World War, but also who scored the goals. He further claimed that he could list all eleven players for each of those matches. I didn't believe him, of course, and initially I exhorted him to stop boasting and concentrate on acquiring some literacy skills.

It turned out that Foxy could do what he claimed, but that only became apparent after I undertook detailed research myself into the recent past of Southampton Football Club. I may be an Arsenal supporter but I was young and committed to my work. With such talent, all the education system could do for Foxy was to give him a stigmatizing label and a measurement that was a gross violation of his real abilities. I can't help feeling that if he had been born into a pre-literate society, he would have been a key figure in passing on its history and culture. I don't know what happened to Foxy but I bet he is not a professor of oral history in one of our universities.

My second personal anomaly came some ten years later just after I had become a lecturer in special educational needs. One of my in-service students worked in a school for the delicate, as it was then called. Within this school many of the children were labelled as autistic (later softened to children with autistic tendencies and, more recently, Asberger's Syndrome) and a small number of these labelled children possessed skills not dissimilar to Foxy's. They could draw with architectural precision, they could memorize music after one hearing, and not just songs, whole symphonies, concertos and the like. Dustin Hoffman portrayed one such person as an adult in the film *Rainman*.

Once again, special education could not bring out the best in these children. It could give them a wholly inappropriate label and attempt to explain their skills by coming up with the pseudo-scientific label 'anomalous representation', whatever that may mean. It could keep them safe and secure but was singly unable to build upon these prodigious talents and develop these children to their full educational and social potential. These children were integrated into the special education paradigm as it was because these talents were labelled as special needs. This also kept the paradigm safe and secure; there was no attempt to question a paradigm that could not explain these wondrous skills.

My third anomaly occurred a few years later. I was a guest speaker at an EEC conference on special education in Holland and as part of the conference I spent a day with several young people with learning difficulties in their group home. It was a very pleasant day, the young people were very welcoming and they discussed their lives and their educational experiences fully and openly. The group home itself was like group homes all over the modern world – clean, comfortable and well designed. But it failed my own personal test of acceptability; I wouldn't have been prepared to live there so I don't think other people should be forced to either.

But that is not the main point I wish to make. What was remarkable about the day was that the language spoken was English. A monolingual senior academic from a university is reliant on six bilingual students who are labelled as having learning difficulties for a satisfactory means of communication. I was visiting their country at their expense as a renowned expert in special education and yet I was completely reliant on them to speak my language. And yet I carried with me the positive academic label 'professor' and they carried with them the essentially negative label 'learning difficulties'. There is surely something anomalous in this.

Personal anomalies, of course, are never enough to produce a paradigm revolution in themselves. It takes what we might call structural or external anomalies to appear as well. The first of these was formally identified by the Warnock Report (1978) when it argued that special education until then had been structured by medical rather than educational need. As a consequence of this, the report's authors argued that the medical classifications that were central to the special education enterprise should be replaced by categories of special educational need. Unfortunately, however, the changes produced in the system as the report's recommendations were implemented were relatively marginal because, although the labels had changed, the practices underpinning them were still based upon an individualized and even still a medicalized model of educational development. Hence, while the report itself may not have produced a revolution, it opened a crack in this particular worldview.

A second structural anomaly was appearing in the special education system as well. Both research and direct experience was revealing systemic biases: proportionately more black children than white were ending up in special education, more working-class than middle-class children and more boys than girls (Mongon, 1982). These biases could only be explained in one of two ways. Either the system was accurately reflecting the different needs of these groups – that is, black children, working-class children and boys had greater special needs than white, middle-class children and girls – or the operation of the special education system was somehow itself responsible for producing these systemic biases. Few people would seriously argue for the former position any more and yet we still have a special educational paradigm that reproduces disadvantage based upon race, gender and class. Nevertheless, this systemic bias remains another and widening crack in the paradigm.

A third structural anomaly centres on the question of whose needs are actually being met by the special education paradigm. Nearly thirty years ago now Sally Tomlinson published a book, *A Sociology of Special Education* (1981), in which she argued that it was not SEN pupils, but those of ordinary schools and the professional staff who work in both special and ordinary education who really benefited from the existence of the special education system. While the book was a fairly traditional neo-Weberian analysis, the application of its ideas to special education caused a furore among special educators and Tomlinson herself was demonized in many gatherings and conferences. Few would now disagree with her central thesis, however: that the special education paradigm serves the interests of a variety of groups, organizations and institutions, only one of which are the children so labelled. So there remains yet another crack in the paradigm; special education is not just about meeting the educational needs of 'special' children.

One of the problems in applying Kuhn's analysis is that it doesn't provide any historical framework in which to locate and even explain why one knowledge paradigm replaces another and why it does so at particular historical moments. These are the issues to which I now need to turn in order to discuss the replacement of the special educational needs paradigm by an inclusive one. In order so to do, I shall briefly discuss the changing relationship between the economy and social policy before going on to discuss the implications that this will have for education in general and special needs education in particular.

The economy and social and educational policy

In discussing the relationship between the economy and education (as well as social) policy we need to bear in mind the point made earlier by Slee (1998), namely that there is a symbiotic relationship between regular and special education. In other words, special education has developed in the ways it has because it has been dependent, by and large, on regular education. While its ideological function has been to educate children whose special needs could not be met in ordinary schools, its real purpose has been to act as a safety valve, taking the children the rest of the system either could not or would not cope with. And there is no doubt that since the coming of schooling for all, social and educational policy has been shaped by capital's need for accumulation and profit, although this is not an attempt to deny that political struggles against inequality and injustice have also played a part. Hence, all social and educational policy can be seen (in part at least) as inextricably linked and shaped by these two competing forces.

As I have already suggested, most social theorists are now in agreement that at present we are in transition from one kind of society to another, although these changes are taking much longer than many of us imagined. If this is the case, and I have already indicated that I think it is, then it is likely that the relationship between the economy and social policy may also change fundamentally. Giddens (1998), for example, suggests that the new welfare state must switch to being a 'risk-management' enterprise whose aim is to prevent problems from occurring rather than one that compensates afterwards. This would obviously involve a renegotiation of the relationship between the economy and social and educational policy; he suggests that the radically reformed welfare state would, in fact be a 'social investment state in the positive welfare society' (*Ibid.*, p. 127).

I think that Giddens is suggesting that the welfare state is changing from being a vehicle for supporting the poor and vulnerable (viz. special education for special children) to becoming a mechanism for encouraging the potentially alienated and disruptive into accepting the responsibilities of citizenship. If Giddens is right, then the implications for special education are indeed profound. Until now the special education paradigm has attempted to compensate individuals for their (presumed) intellectual, physical or behavioural deficits although, as I and others have already suggested, it has failed. We have seen a variety of attempts by special education post-Warnock to create active citizens out of their children but with little indication of success.

Inevitably, then, the goals of social and educational policy are already in the process of changing in the society to which we are moving. Historically, the main goals of educational and social policy have been to produce a healthy and compliant workforce and a social division of labour that reproduced this. Leaving aside the odd difficulty caused by the boom-and-bust trade cycle, by and large educational and social policy delivered these goals very well. However, it is becoming increasing obvious that, with the rise of the global economy and higher productivity due to new technology, these conditions are changing fast. What this means is that fewer people work to produce more goods and hence the goals of the current state are not so much concerned with the supply of labour and social reproduction as with the demand for goods worldwide and the need to control the ever-increasing non-working population.

This, I would suggest, will inevitably mean that the relationship between the economy and social and educational policy will need to change fundamentally to address these different goals:

> Social policy in such conditions is conceived less as a means to redistribute incomes and wealth, or to act as a band-aid for capitalism, and rather as a means of increasing individual opportunities by creating labour market flexibility in a global economy and expanding the non-inflationary growth rate of the British economy. (Driver and Martell, 1999, p. 250)

Undoubtedly, this will have profound implications for social policy in general and education policy in particular. It is the magnitude of some of these changes that will be discussed in the next section.

Work and education in the changing world

As the nature of work changes it is inevitable that the relationship between work and education will change as well. This is bound to have a major impact on education. As Kerzner Lipsky and Gartner put it, 'Just as the regime of the production line influenced the shape of public education in the industrial era, the nature of post-industrial society and its work have consequences for the educational system of the twenty first century' (Kerzner Lipsky and Gartner, 1997, p. 250).

Under these conditions education can no longer function to serve the needs of the capitalist nation state.

The reasons for this are becoming increasingly obvious. First, we are seeing the rise of the global economy in which both the size and power of multi-national companies are beginning to supersede the nation state. As a consequence these multi-nationals have a presence in education systems with their sponsorship schemes buying books, computers and other equipment and funding research and scholarship. Second, the global economy is increasingly being driven by consumption rather than production, making the rationale for these sponsorship schemes obvious; their corporate imagery penetrates deeper and deeper into ever-younger minds. Finally, flexible labour markets are becoming increasingly internationalized, posing difficulties for national education systems. As more and more young people come to realize that their futures have been exported, they increasingly vote with their feet and abandon their schools for the shopping malls and the streets.

Given these far-reaching and fundamental changes that are now occurring in the economy, it is obvious that the relationship between it and education will also change fundamentally. But, more importantly for our purposes here, if these changes are indeed occurring, then there is bound to be a considerable impact on special education itself. Before going on to consider this in some detail, we need to examine the evidence we already have for changes in the relationship between education and the economy that are beginning to occur.

One obvious change as we move into the twenty-first century is that fewer people are working to support more people who don't. This is reproduced in education, where the numbers of people studying full and part time are far greater than they have ever been. Additionally, we see governments supporting a whole range of 'education for life' initiatives which acknowledge that the old relationship between education and the economy has broken down; schooling no longer ends when adolescents have been prepared for jobs for life. 'Governments need to emphasise "life long education", developing education programmes that start from an individual's early years and continue on even late in life' (Giddens, 1998, p. 125). A further change has seen the increasing marketization of education and a move away from the ideology of 'education for personal growth' and towards education serving the needs of flexible international labour markets and the global economy. Another change is occurring in the education curriculum, in schools as well as further and higher education. It is being driven increasingly by other kinds of normative criteria such as standard assessment tests

(SATS) of one kind or another and this is in spite of the fact that in recent years we have seen the development of sustained critiques of the normative criteria, such as IQ testing, on which education has previously been based.

A final change is the increasing importance that national politicians give to education; they still see votes for education as key to their election. So in the 1997 general election in Britain, when Tony Blair was asked to list his three priorities for government, he replied 'education, education, education'. Education has continued to be given high priority by successive governments. This usually results in paper chases to obtain educational qualifications for jobs where such qualifications are not necessary because, as Jordan has pointed out, 'it is a complete fallacy to suppose a correlation between high standards in education and technical training and high levels of economic participation' (Jordan, 1998, p. 47).

The changes outlined above are not all in the same direction, of course, and they often contradict each other. This apparently contradictory set of 'social facts' is relatively easy to explain. We are straddling the shift from one kind of society to another and under such circumstances we can expect to see a battle between conservative and radical forces. Indeed, the German sociologist Karl Mannheim (1936) drew attention to this in a book tellingly entitled *Ideology and Utopia*. More recently, other writers have turned to this and Jock Young has called the phenomenon 'the contradictions of late modernity'. Using a nautical metaphor, he explains:

> The movement into late modernity is like a ship which has broken from its moorings. Many of the crew try to return to the familiar sanctuary of the harbour but to their alarm the compass spins, the ship continues on its way and, looking back, the quay is no longer secure: at times it seems to be falling apart, its structure fading and disintegrating. The siren voices which forlornly, seriously, soberly try to convince them that going back is possible are mistaken. (Young, 1999, p. 191)

Special education at the crossroads

So what does all this mean for special education? If education is going to be fundamentally changed in the new society to which we are moving and going back is impossible, then it is also inevitable that special education will be transformed, indeed if it is to survive at all. Special education does not exist in some kind of privileged vacuum that will keep it immune from these changes because 'There can be no disputing that the history of special education is inseparable from the history of regular education' (Richardson, 1999, p. xv). In fact, we can begin to see from the struggles already being waged over the role and future of special education that it will be transformed by some of the major social and economic forces I have outlined in this chapter. The way in which debates in special education have moved away from what used to be called the integration/segregation debate and onto what has come to be called the inclusion/exclusion debate is indicative of the fact that this debate, once narrowly confined to education is now about the possibility of the inclusive society (Oliver, 1996b). And with the coming of the idea of the inclusive society, special education, which has excluded throughout its history, faces the possibility of its own exclusion.

Of course, it is possible to argue, as Roger Slee does, that this shift 'connotes a linguistic adjustment to present a politically correct façade to a changing world' (Slee, 1998, p. 131). While this may be the case for many within special education, I would argue that the implications of this changing world are so profound that mere linguistic adjustment is a strategy that is bound to fail those special educators wishing to keep things as they are. And for the remainder of this paper, I do not wish to concentrate on those reactionary, conservative forces that promote such a strategy, but instead, to focus on the radical, transformative potential that may emerge from some of the struggles beginning to take place in and over special education.

Writing ourselves back into history

The changes in society identified earlier are just as apparent in the arena of human agency as they are in other aspects of our worlds. On the one hand, we see the decline of traditional political institutions like monarchies, states and parties and yet, on the other, we see a plethora of disempowered and disenfranchised groups organizing themselves into new social movements of all kinds. These movements often cross national boundaries, present broadly based critiques of existing economic, political and social institutions and arrangements and use a whole range of tactics to promote their ideas and goals. However, it has to be admitted that these movements have not been as successful as many of us thought. Further, traditional political institutions have shown a resilient capacity to integrate these agendas into their own programmes; for example, many of the issues of the green movement are now being promoted by all political parties as central parts of their programmes.

Special education is not immune from the effects of these new social movements. It is not changing just because of the anomalies in its paradigm, nor is it being changed only by the broader economic and social forces that are transforming all our lives. It is also being transformed by the dissenting voices of disabled people and others who have promoted the idea of the inclusive society. With the rise of a powerful international disabled people's movement, the critical voices of disabled people have begun to speak out against our incarceration in all areas of our lives and the institutions in which we have been placed; whether those institutions be residential homes, hospitals, villages, special schools or units. But the radical forces for inclusion have also been confronted by equally powerful forces for exclusion; in the case of special education, as the demands for inclusion have become louder so have the demands to preserve special schools, orchestrated by overstretched teachers, unions, some parents groups and special schools themselves.

These struggles in special education have not been merely positional or locational; that is, about where and how to educate children with special needs. They have also taken place at the ideological or cultural level and have been about whether we need to celebrate or control difference. Of course, the contradictions of late modernity cannot be ignored here either; with the emergence of the radical forces of celebration we have also seen the coming of the conservative forces of eradication. For disabled people, the potential for celebration as society changes is, at least, tempered by the threats of genetic engineering, selective abortion, non-resuscitation policies, health care rationing and euthanasia.

In these increasingly intense struggles between conservative and radical forces, standing still is not an option for special education. If the forces of reaction emerge triumphant, society will not continue to fund special places for special people because the economic returns will not justify it and eradication will be the preferred option. If the forces of radicalism emerge triumphant, there will simply be no place for special education in the inclusive society. The final question for this paper, therefore, is, who will win?

Conclusions – does special education have a future?

As far as special education is concerned, as I have argued herein, standing still is not an option because change is coming anyway. At the beginning, I referred to a previous keynote address I had given in Ireland. At the end of that conference, I was asked how I felt that people had responded to my suggestion that special education had no future. My response was that the tide of history was about to sweep over special education and that I had met with three kinds of response. The first were what I called 'ostriches'; people who thought that they could bury their heads in the sand and let the tide sweep over them. The second were a group I called the 'rubber ducks' or, to borrow Slee's term, the 'linguistic adjusters'; they were a group who thought they could bob around on the tide of history but remain untouched. The third group I called the 'surfers'; they saw the incoming tide as a challenge not just to be faced but also to be ridden to a better place while enjoying the buzz that surfing brings.

Special education has no choice; it can begin to change itself from within or be swept away by the tide of history that is washing over us all in the twenty-first century. It can be part of the struggle to produce a more inclusive world or it can continue to align itself with the forces of exclusion. The former strategy offers us all the possibility of a decent future, the latter offers a few of us the illusion of a safe and stable world. I hope that special education is mature enough to make the right choice.

Section 2

Theorizing and Changing a Disabling World

6

Disability and Normalization: A Critique

The concept of normalization was first introduced in Scandinavia in the 1960s as an attempt to improve the lives of people who were then referred to as the mentally handicapped in Europe and the mentally retarded in North America. The vast majority of this group were segregated from society, either living in large institutions or isolated within their own families. The basic idea behind the concept was that services should be aimed enabling these people to lead ordinary lives living, learning and working in their own communities. While this idea seemed sensible and humanitarian and was quickly seized upon by politicians, policy-makers and professionals worried by emerging scandals over abuse in long-stay institutions, it also became somewhat controversial. The idea somehow got translated into policies aimed at trying to 'make people normal' with all that implies. So controversial did this become that in North America the basic idea was changed into giving people 'normal social roles' and normalization itself became social role valorization (SRV).

My first encounter with normalization was in the 1970s. I was invited with a number of other disabled people to the King's Fund Centre in London to attend a workshop promoting the normalization principle as a potential way of delivering services for disabled people in general and the mentally handicapped (as people with learning difficulties were then usually called in Britain, though the normalizers at the conference preferred mental retardation). Their founder, Wolf Wolfensberger, was not in attendance, but his colleagues subjected us to a constant stream of highly contentious and sometimes disabling comments about disabled people and the services we were supposed to need. This would have been fine in itself because the normalizers were not the first nor will they be the last to distort our experiences and tell us what we ought to want from services, but all this was presented as scientific fact and there was no scope within the workshop programme for challenging or confronting them.

I have to confess that I, and some of the other disabled people present, behaved rather badly after our attempts to open a dialogue were summarily rejected; we provided a series of loud interruptions from the back in an attempt to disrupt the programme. When this was to no avail we noisily left the workshop before the end. This did not, however, signal the end of the normalization workshops and over the next few years many took place all over Britain. It is my understanding that in these workshops too, there was little room to challenge the principles and practice of what had now become social role valorization and, indeed, workshops continued until all the participants had fully internalized the ideas and values being promoted. Precisely what influence these ideas and values had on subsequent service development depends on your point of view and I, of course, would argue that it has been negligible.

My next encounter was with Wolf Wolfensberger himself at a conference organized by Len Barton in Bristol in 1988. We were both keynote speakers; I presented a paper which sketched out some of the ideas I was working on for my book *The Politics of Disablement* (1990) and Wolfensberger presented a very interesting paper on what he called 'human services', arguing that their real purpose was to provide employment for the middle classes rather than support for the vulnerable. From this I assumed he had moved away from social role valorization and was now subjecting human services to welcome critical scrutiny. Hence, I was surprised a few years later to receive an invitation to present a keynote address at a conference in Canada celebrating twenty-five years of social role valorization. My initial response was that I didn't think that twenty-five years of SRV was much to celebrate and I would be highly critical of it and its claims. The organizers assured me that they wanted a critical perspective and that was why I had been invited, so I accepted the invitation.

At the conference I was made to feel very welcome and was treated very well. However, the atmosphere at the conference was much more like a religious revivalist meeting than any academic conference I had ever attended. The responses of participants at the conference to my paper could be divided into two camps: most ignored my ideas completely, but some offered to convert me to the faith – usually in private, however, where I could be 're-educated' into the values of social role valorization. Wolfensberger himself dismissed my presentation, both from the platform and later in a written response, as religious ideology, professing that he could only deal with the ideas of science. Given the atmosphere and tone of the conference, I have often wondered since whether he was being ironic or even mischievous but I think he was serious. What follows is the paper I gave at the conference, which later appeared in an edited book of the proceedings (Flynn and Lemay, 1999).

~~~~~~~~~~

Capitalism, disability and ideology: a materialist critique of the normalization principle

Introduction

At the outset, I should say two things. I have no particular interest in the history of normalization and, therefore, I am not attempting to provide a revisionist history of it. Neither do I think that normalization, or social role valorization as it has become in its reincarnation, has much to offer in developing a social theory of disability. I am interested, however, in the oppression of disabled people in capitalist societies and what normalization does, or rather does not, say about it.

This interest has led me to begin to sketch out what a social theory of disability might look like (Oliver, 1990). For me, all social theory must be judged on three interrelated elements: its adequacy in describing experience; its ability to explain experience; and, finally, its potential to transform experience. My own theorizing on disability is located in Marxist political economy which, I would argue, offers a much more adequate basis for describing and explaining experience than does normalization theory, which is based upon interactionist and functionalist sociology.

In fact, I would go further and argue that the social theory that underpins Marxist political economy has far greater transformative potential in eradicating the oppression that disabled people face throughout the world than the interactionist and functionalist theories that underpin normalization ever can have. And I will go even further than that and argue that already this theory has had a far greater influence on the struggles that disabled people are themselves currently engaged in to remove the chains of that oppression than normalization, which is, at best, a bystander in these struggles and, at worst, part of the process of oppression itself.

In presenting this argument, I will begin by articulating my own theoretical position based upon Marxist political economy and hereinafter
referred to as materialist theory. I will then demonstrate the inadequacies of normalization theory's explanation of the rise of the institution
before going on to provide a critique of the ideology that underpins it.
Next, I will take issue with the argument that normalization has been
successful because it is based upon 'experience'. Finally, I will look
at what both normalization and materialist theories say about change,
having briefly described the appalling material conditions under which
disabled people live throughout the world.

Before proceeding further, it is perhaps necessary to explain the
use of terminology in this chapter. Underpinning it is a materialist
view of society; to say that the category 'disability' is produced by
capitalist society in a particular form implies a particular worldview.
Within this worldview, the production of the category disability is no
different from the production of motor cars or hamburgers. Each has
an industry, whether it be the car, fast food or human service industry.
Each industry has a workforce that has a vested interest in producing
their product in particular ways and in exerting as much control over
the process of production as possible.

The production of disability therefore is nothing more or less than a
set of activities specifically geared towards producing a good – the category disability – supported by a range of political actions, which create
the conditions to allow these productive activities to take place, and
underpinned by a discourse that gives legitimacy to the whole enterprise. As to the specifics of the terminology used in this discourse,
I use the term 'disabled people' generically and refuse to divide the
group in terms of medical conditions, functional limitation or severity
of impairment. For me, disabled people are defined in terms of three
criteria: (1) they have an impairment; (2) they experience oppression as a consequence; and (3) they identify themselves as a disabled
person.

Using the generic term does not mean that I do not recognize
differences in experience within the group but that in exploring this we
should start from the ways oppression differentially impacts on different
groups of people rather than with differences in experience among
individuals with different impairments. I agree that my own initial
outlining of a materialist theory of disability (Oliver, 1990) did not
specifically include an examination of the oppression that people with
learning difficulties face (and I use this particular term throughout my

paper because it is the one democratic and accountable organizations of people with learning difficulties insist on).

Nevertheless I agree that, 'For a rigorous theory of disability to emerge which begins to examine all disability in a materialist account, an analysis of normalization must be included' (Chappell, 1992, p. 38). Attempting to incorporate normalization in a materialist account, however, does not mean that I believe that, beyond the descriptive, it is of much use. Based as it is upon functionalist and interactionist sociology, whose defects are well known (Gouldner, 1975), it offers no satisfactory explanation of why disabled people are oppressed in capitalist societies and no strategy for liberating us from the chains of that oppression.

Political economy, on the other hand, suggests that all phenomena (including social categories) are produced by the economic and social forces of capitalism itself. The forms in which they are produced are ultimately dependent upon their relationship to the economy (Marx, 1913). Hence, the category disability is produced in the particular form it appears by these very economic and social forces. Further, it is produced as an economic problem because of changes in the nature of work and the needs of the labour market within capitalism. 'The speed of factory work, the enforced discipline, the time-keeping and production norms – all these were a highly unfavourable change from the slower, more self-determined methods of work into which many handicapped people had been integrated' (Ryan and Thomas, 1980, p. 101). The economy, through both the operation of the labour market and the social organization of work, plays a key role in producing the category disability and in determining societal responses to disabled people. In order to explain this further, it is necessary to return to the crucial question of what is meant by political economy. The following is a generally agreed definition of political economy:

> the study of the interrelationships between the polity, economy and society, or more specifically, the reciprocal influences among government the economy, social classes, state and status groups. The central problem of the political economy perspective is the manner in which the economy and polity interact in a relationship of reciprocal causation affecting the distribution of social goods. (Estes, Swan and Gerard, 1982, p. 47)

The central problem with such an agreed definition is that it is an explanation that can be incorporated into pluralist visions of society as a consensus emerging out of the interests of various groups and social forces and, indeed, this explanation has been encapsulated as follows:

> A person's position in society affects the type and severity of physical disability one is likely to experience and more importantly the likelihood that he or she is likely to receive rehabilitation services. Indeed, the political economy of a community dictates what debilitating health conditions will be produced, how and under what circumstances they will be defined, and ultimately who will receive the services. (Albrecht, 1992, p. 14)

This quote lays out the way in which Albrecht pursues his argument in three parts. The first part shows how the kind of society in which people live influences the kinds of disability that are produced, notably how the mode of production creates particular kinds of impairments. Further, he traces the ways in which the mode of production influences social interpretation and the meanings of disability and he also demonstrates how, in industrial societies, rehabilitation, like all other goods and services, is transformed into a commodity. The second part of the argument shows how intermediate social institutions in America, such as the legal, the political and welfare systems, contribute to the specific way in which disability is produced and comments on their role in the transformation of rehabilitation into a commodity. The final part considers what this may mean in terms of future developments in social policy and what effects it may have on the lives of disabled people.

It is difficult to disagree with this formulation at the descriptive level, but the problem with this pluralist version of political economy is that the structure of capitalist America itself goes unexamined as does the crucial role that the capitalist economy plays in shaping the experience of groups and individuals. Exactly the same criticism can be levelled at normalization theory. Devaluation according to normalization theory is a universal cognitive process and economic and social conditions are only relevant to who gets devalued.

Political economy, as it is used here, takes a particular theoretical view of society; one which sees the economy as the crucial and, ultimately, determining factor, in structuring the lives of groups and individuals. Further, while the relationship between various groups and the economy may differ in qualitative ways, the underlying structural relationship remains:

> The convergence and interaction of liberating forces at work in society against racism, sexism, ageism and economic imperialism are all oppressive 'isms' and

built-in responses of a society that considers certain groups inferior. All are rooted in the social-economic structures of society. All deprive certain groups of status, the right to control their own lives and destinies with the end result of powerlessness. All have resulted in economic and social discrimination. All rob (American) society of the energies and involvement of creative persons who are needed to make our society just and humane. All have brought on individual alienation, despair, hostility, and anomie. (Walton, 1979, p. 9)

Hence, the oppression that disabled people face is rooted in the economic and social structures of capitalism. And this oppression is structured by racism, sexism, homophobia, ageism and disablism, which are endemic to all capitalist societies, and cannot be explained away as a universal cognitive process. To explain this further it is necessary to go back to the roots of capitalism itself.

Disabled people and the rise of capitalism

Whatever the fate of disabled people before the advent of capitalist society and whatever their fate will be in the brave new world of the twenty-first century, with its coming we suffered economic and social exclusion. As a consequence of this exclusion, disability was produced in a particular form; as an individual problem requiring medical treatment.

At the heart of this exclusion was the institution – something on which we would all agree. In the nineteenth and twentieth centuries, institutions proliferated in all industrial societies (Rothman, 1971), but to describe this, as Wolfensberger does, as 'momentum without rationale' (p. 3) is patently absurd. The French Marxist, Louis Althusser (1971), suggested that all capitalist societies are faced with the problem of social control and they resolve this by a combination of repressive and ideological mechanisms.

The reason for the success of the institution was simple; it combines these mechanisms almost perfectly. It is repressive in that all those who either cannot or will not conform to the norms and discipline of capitalist society can be removed from it. It is ideological in that it stands as a visible monument for all those who currently conform but may not continue to do so – if you do not behave, the institution awaits you.

It is for this reason that the institution has been successful. Its presence perfectly meets capitalism's needs for discipline and control (Foucault, 1972). It is also the reason why, despite the fact that the defects of institutions have been known for the 200 years that they have existed, they have remained unaddressed. Indeed, the principle of 'less eligibility' was central to the rise of the institution. It is simply not true to say that we have only known of their defects in recent years because, if this were the case, they would then not have been performing their ideological control function. Day trips to institutions, which originated in the 1850s not the 1950s, were precisely for this purpose; to demonstrate how awful they were for the purposes of social control, not to educate the public about their reform.

What is also not in dispute between us is that, in the second half of the twentieth century, the physical and ideological dominance of the institution began to decline (Scull, 1977). What is in dispute, however, is why this should be so. While not claiming that the normalization principle was the only causal factor in what has become known as de-institutionalization or de-carceration, Wolfensberger nonetheless claims that it 'broke the back of the institutional movement' (p. 60) and without it 'there would have been massive investments in building new, smaller, regionalised institutions' (p. 16). I would not wish to dismiss the role of ideas, or more appropriately, ideologies in this process, but there were other, more important factors.

Most importantly, the rising costs of institutional care were becoming a major factor in the shift to community-based care. Ideology was turned into political action when this, along with other factors such as rising oil prices, spiralling arms expenditure and so on, brought about fiscal crises in many capitalist states (O'Connor, 1973; Gough, 1979). This fiscal crisis explanation stands in stark contrast to Wolfensberger's (1989, p. 36) assertion that while de-institutionalization may have started in the 1950s, it was a 'drift that occurred without much planning, intent or consciousness'.

The transition to late capitalism (the post-industrial society, as some writers have called it, or its more recent fashionable manifestation as postmodernity) has seen this process continue apace. The question it raises is, what does this process mean? Cohen suggests that it

> is thought by some to represent a questioning, even a radical reversal of that earlier transformation, by others merely to signify a continuation and intensification of its patterns. (Cohen, 1985, p. 13)

Those who have promoted the idea of normalization would, I suspect, place themselves in the first camp. That is to say, the move from the institution to the community is part of a process of removing some of the apparatus of social control by the state. I would place myself in the latter camp, seeing this move as an extension of the processes of control within the capitalist state.

After all, the balance of power between disabled people and professionals has not changed at all. The situation described by Cohen (1985) remains unchanged:

> much the same groups of experts are doing much the same business as usual. The basic rituals incorporated into the move to the mind – taking case histories, writing social enquiry reports, constructing files, organising case conferences – are still being enacted. (Cohen, 1985, p. 152)

In the world of late capitalism, the same people, albeit with different jobs titles and perhaps in plusher buildings, are doing the same things to disabled people, although they may now be calling them 'doing a needs-led assessment' or 'producing a care plan' in Britain. Elsewhere it may be called individual programme planning, social brokerage, change agentry and the like. But the material fact remains, it is still professionals doing it, whatever 'it' is called, to disabled people.

All social changes require an ideology to support the economic rationality underpinning them. So the ideology underpinning the rise of the institution was ultimately a medical and a therapeutic one; accordingly placing people in institutions was not only good for the health of individuals, it was also good for the health of society. Normalization, it could be argued, is the ideology (or one of the ideologies) that allowed people to be returned to the community in that they can be 'normalized' or, in its later variant, be allocated normal (valued) social roles. After all, we don't want the different, the deviant or even the dangerous returned to our communities.

I fully realize that here I am stepping on dangerous ground and that both Wolfensberger (1994) and Nirje (1993) would probably argue that I am confusing normal with normalization. There is not the space to demonstrate that I realize that this is not the case, nor to draw attention to their own published ambiguities on this issue. Instead, I wish to point out that normalization is part of a discourse that is predicated on the normal/abnormal distinction and it is certainly clear that Wolfensberger thinks this distinction is real rather than socially constructed.

A materialist approach to this would suggest, as does the French philosopher Foucault (1973), that the way we talk about the world and the way we experience it are inextricably linked – the names we give to things shapes our experience of them and our experience of things in the world influences the names we give to them. Hence, our practices of normalizing people and normalizing services both construct and maintain the normal/abnormal dichotomy.

It is becoming clear that the social structures of late capitalist societies cannot be discussed in a discourse of normality/abnormality because what characterizes them is difference; differences based on gender, ethnic backgrounds, sexual orientation, abilities, religious beliefs, wealth, age, access or non-access to work and so on. And in societies founded on oppression, these differences cross-cut and intersect each other in ways we haven't even begun to properly understand, let alone try to resolve (Zarb and Oliver, 1993).

The concept of simultaneous oppression (Stuart, 1992) may offer a more adequate way of understanding differences within the generic category of disability. Certainly people are beginning to talk about their experience in this way:

> As a black disabled woman, I cannot compartmentalise or separate aspects of my identity in this way. The collective experience of my race, disability and gender are what shape and inform my life. (Hill, 1994, p. 7)

Kirsten Hearn provides a poignant account of how disabled lesbians and gay men are excluded from all their potential communities. First,

> The severely able-bodied community and straight disabled community virtually ignored our campaign, (Hearn, 1991, p. 30)

and

> Issues of equality are not fashionable for the majority of the severely able-bodied, white, middle-class lesbian and gay communities. (Hearn, 1991, p. 33)

The point that I am making is that the discourse of normalization (whatever the intent of its major proponents and however badly they feel it has been misused by its disciples) can never adequately describe or explain societies characterized by difference because of its reductionist views of both humanity and society. Individual and group differences cannot be described solely in terms of the normality/abnormality dichotomy and inegalitarian social structures cannot be explained by reference only to valued and devalued social roles. Normalization can also never serve to transform peoples lives; a point to which I shall return.

The role of experience

In explaining why the idea of normalization was so powerful for many people, Wolfensberger (1994) claims that it connected with their common sense, it gave them a language or discourse in which to talk about the issues and it gave them a unified mental scheme (social theory) connecting a range of issues. Of course, in talking about this he is talking about the connection of these ideas to the experience of academics, professionals and policy-makers, not to the experience of people with learning difficulties.

He also claims that 'a single theory or principle could be applied to all; not only to all retarded people and not only to all handicapped people but to all deviant ones' (Wolfensberger, 1994, p. 58). I remember attending the first conference on normalization in Britain in the mid-1970s when such claims were made. Vic Finkelstein and myself vociferously denied the claim that the half-digested mishmash of functionalist and interactionist sociology we were being presented with had anything to do with our experiences as disabled people.

Our claims were of course denied, as they often have been in the past, on the grounds that as isolated, elite disabled individuals, our experiences did not accord with those of the majority of disabled people (a basis on which you may wish to deny my claims in this chapter). And, of course, the normalization bandwagon rolled on in Britain, into social service departments, health authorities and undemocratic voluntary organizations; but not into the newly emerging democratic and accountable organizations that disabled people were setting up at the time. To this day, not a single one of these organizations of disabled people has adopted the normalization principle as the basis for its operations or as a rationale for its existence.

Our experiences at that conference mirrored our experience in terms of disability politics more generally. We were already being told by groups of able-bodied experts that not only did they know best what our problems were, they also knew best how to solve them. As disabled people we were developing our own views both on those experts who wished to define or colonize our experience and to identify what our problems really were. These views were encapsulated in 'a little red book' called *Fundamental Principles of Disability* (UPIAS, 1976), which, I would argue, is far more important for disabled people than all the publications on normalization put together.

This slim volume is not widely available but the debt that disabled people owe to it is enormous. I, and many other disabled people, openly acknowledge our debt to the document in the way it shaped our own understanding of disability (Oliver, 1995). The document has never been widely available and with the demise of the Union in 1991, it will become increasingly difficult to obtain. I reproduce two passages here, the first of which exposes the role of 'experts' in our lives and the second of which defines our own problems for us:

> The Union maintains that, far from being too concerned with the cause of disability, the 'experts' in the field have never concerned themselves with the real cause at all. The fact that they had delusions that they were looking at the cause, when they were typically concentrating on its effects, on confusing disability with physical impairment, underlines the imperative need for disabled people to become their own experts. It is only when we begin to grasp this expertise that disabled people will be able to see through the 'experts' attempt to disguise as something 'entirely different' the traditional, clearly failed, 'spontaneous' struggle against aspects of disability, such as poverty.
>
> Disability is something imposed on top of our impairments by the way we are unnecessarily isolated and excluded from full participation in society. Disabled people are therefore an oppressed group in society. To understand this it is necessary to grasp the distinction between the physical impairment and the social situation, called 'disability', of people with such impairment. Thus we define impairment as lacking part of or all of a limb, or having a defective limb, organ or mechanism of the body; and disability as the disadvantage or restriction of activity caused by a contemporary social organisation which takes no or little account of people who have physical impairments and thus excludes them from participation in the mainstream of social activities. Physical disability is therefore a particular form of social oppression. (UPIAS, 1976, p. 14)

It was from this work that I and a number of other disabled people began to write and talk about the social model of disability. For my own part I originally conceptualized models of disability as the binary distinction between what I chose to call the individual and social models of disability (Oliver, 1983). This was no amazing new insight on my part dreamed up in some ivory tower, but was really an attempt to enable me to make sense of the world for the social work students and other professionals who I was teaching at the time. The idea of the individual and the social model was taken quite simply and explicitly from the distinction originally made between impairment and disability by the Union of the Physically Impaired Against Segregation in the *Fundamental Principles* document (1976).

The articulation of this new view of disability did not receive universal acceptance. Originally, it was professionals, policy-makers and staff from organizations for disabled people who, because they had vested interests in maintaining the status quo underpinned by the individual model, questioned the experiential validity and explanatory reliability of the social model. However, we have seen a paradigm shift and many professional bodies and groups have now come to espouse the social model, in theory at least (DHSS, 1988; Gillespie-Sells and Campbell, 1991). Whether it has had much impact on professional practice is another question altogether and beyond the scope of this paper.

The articulation of the social model was received much more enthusiastically by disabled people because it made an immediate connection to their own experiences. It quickly became the basis for disability awareness and later disability equality training. It was adopted by democratic disability organizations all over the world, including Disabled Peoples International (DPI) and the British Council of Organizations of Disabled People (BCODP), and remains as central to their rationale.

In reading Wolfensberger's comments about how the whole normalization enterprise came about, I am struck by just how much in the way of economic resources (plane tickets, hotel bookings, secretarial support, etc.) went in to producing it. Similarly, the World Health Organization has spent millions of pounds, dollars and yen on trying to describe and classify us (Wood, 1980) and has lamentably failed.

Disabled people, whose intellectual labours have produced the social model, have done this without access to the kinds of resources available to international academic superstars, professionals and policy-makers, as well as the usual coterie of hangers-on and free-loaders. Imagine how much farther down the road we might be if disabled people had been given these resources to develop our own social theory, our own quality measures for human services and our own classification schemes.

The material conditions of disabled people throughout the world

Developing materialist theory in respect of disability requires us to understand the material conditions under which disabled people live throughout the world. A report by the United Nations has confirmed earlier estimates that there are more than 500 million impaired persons in the world; that is, one in ten of the world's population. The report goes on to suggest that at least '25 per cent of the entire population is adversely affected by the presence of disabilities'(Despouy, 1991, p. 1).

There have been very few international studies of the lives of disabled people, although the UN report did come to the following conclusion:

> these persons frequently live in deplorable conditions, owing to the presence of physical and social barriers which prevent their integration and full participation in the community. As a result, millions of disabled people throughout

the world are segregated and deprived of virtually all their rights, and lead a
wretched, marginal life. (Despouy, 1991, p. 1)

It is possible to put some descriptive flesh on the bones of these figures and what follows relies heavily on figures presented in a recent
special edition of the *New Internationalist* (no. 233/July 1992) called
'Disabled Lives'. Of the 500 million disabled people in the world,
300 million live in developing countries, and of these 140 million
are children. One in five, that is 100 million of the total population
of disabled people, are disabled by malnutrition. In the developing
countries, only one in a hundred disabled people have access to any
form of rehabilitation and 80 per cent of all disabled people live in
Asia and the Pacific, but they receive just 2 per cent of the total
resources allocated to disabled people. In the Third World, the death
rate of people with a spinal injury within two years of the injury is
as high today as it was in the developed world before the Second
World War.

While not being able to put an accurate figure onto it, there is no
doubt that, all over the world, there is a close link between disability
and poverty:

> There is a close relationship between poverty and disability: malnutrition,
> mothers weakened by frequent childbirth, inadequate immunisation pro-
> grammes, accidents in over crowded homes, all contribute to an incidence
> of disability among poor people that is higher than among people living in
> easier circumstances. Furthermore, disability creates and exacerbates poverty
> by increasing isolation and economic strain, not just for the individual but for
> the family: there is little doubt that disabled people are amongst the poorest in
> poor countries. (Coleridge, 1993, p. 64)

While, in an absolute sense, the material conditions of disabled people
in the developed world are vastly superior to their Third World counterparts, they still experience conditions of life far inferior to the rest of
the population. Thus, for example, more than 60 per cent of disabled
people in both Britain and America currently live below the poverty
line.

Labour markets in the developed world continue to discriminate
to the point where disabled people are three times more likely to be
unemployed than their able-bodied counterparts. In education, the
majority of disabled children are still educated in segregated special
schools and less than three in a thousand disabled students end up in
higher education, when, according to prevalence figures, it should be

one hundred. On any indicators, disabled women and black disabled people fare worse than their white, male counterparts.

While, the accuracy of some of these figures might be called into question in respect of both the developed and developing world, no one would deny that they paint an authentic picture of the lives of disabled people throughout the world. The point at issue is what can be done about producing the necessary changes. In the next section, I shall discuss the different positions of normalization and materialist theories in respect of producing changes in the lives of disabled people.

Economic, political and social change – how will it be delivered?

In comparing what normalization and materialist theory have to offer in respect of these changes, I want to concentrate on three inter-related areas: change in individuals, change in social policy and welfare programmes and change through the political process.

Partly, I suspect, because of the unacknowledged impact that the social model has had, both Nirje and Wolfensberger are anxious to claim that normalization does not mean making individuals normal. They go further and suggest that it can be applied even more fruitfully to environments. Wolfensberger, however, honestly admits that:

> as long as one grants that abnormalization abnormalizes a person, and not just the person's environment, one cannot say that normalization only normalizes life conditions ... In short I cannot see how Nirje's formulation allows an exclusion of actions on a person. (Wolfensberger, 1994, p. 97)

It is the final sentence that raises issues of grave concern. The history of oppression is underpinned by allowing 'actions on persons' and the crucial questions this raises are: who decides, what actions and which persons? To answer, as normalization does, that prevailing life conditions, environments and values are the ones into which to normalize individuals, begs huge questions and may take us down the road to death-making, sterilization, physical torture, incarceration and mind control. This list is part of our collective history as disabled people, as we are beginning to discover as we begin to write this history, and not some emotive or exaggerated imagining to make a political point (Morris, 1991; Coleridge, 1993).

Materialist theory does not have the same problem with changing individuals, although it is their consciousness that it wants to change, not their bodies, their behaviour or their social roles. Transforming consciousness is a matter of changing personal experiences into political issues. This materialist theory does, and it also links the two; at the collective level disabled people may 'false consciously' believe that the difficulties they face are because of their individual impairments. Hence, they 'internalize oppression' (Sutherland, 1981; Morris, 1991) by believing that it is their fault that they cannot get a job, use public transport and so on. Social and individual transformations are inextricably linked. However, in materialist theory individuals must transform themselves through collective action, not be transformed by others who know what's best for them or what's best for society.

Empowerment is a collective process of transformation on which the powerless embark as part of the struggle to resist the oppression of others, as part of their demands to be included, and/or to articulate their own views of the world. Central to this struggle is the recognition by the powerless that they are oppressed, first articulated in respect of disability by the Union of the Physically Impaired Against Segregation in the 1970s and more recently given a theoretical reformulation within 'oppression theory' more generally (Abberley, 1987).

Normalization theory sees improving human services as a major platform for improving the quality of life for disabled people and, indeed, much time and energy is devoted to precisely this. Wolfensberger's position on this is unequivocal; he is vehemently opposed to services provided by institutions but has spent much of his working life developing and improving community-based services. As I suggested earlier, this is because he views community-based services as radically different from institutional ones in that they are not part of the social control apparatus of the state.

While his position on community-based human services may be unequivocal, it is certainly contradictory. In the paper he gave at the international disability conference in Bristol in 1987, he came very close to taking a materialist position on all human services, not simply institutional ones, when he argued that their real purpose (latent function) was to provide employment for the middle classes and in order to continue to do that:

> merely enlarging the human service empire is not sufficient to meet all the requirements that a post-primary production economy poses. In addition, one has to make all the services that do exist as unproductive as possible – indeed one has to make them counterproductive if at all possible, so that they create dependency, and so that they create impaired people rather than habilitate them. (Wolfensberger, 1989, p. 34)

The problem with this formulation is that it mistakes the symptom for the problem. If human services under capitalism are part of the state apparatus of social control, as materialist theory would argue, the reason they employ the middle classes is simple: they are not the groups who pose a threat to capitalism and, therefore, they do not need to be controlled, but instead can become agents for the control of others.

It is precisely for this reason that the demands of disabled people all over the world are not, any longer, for improvements in existing services but control over them. And, further, their struggles around welfare issues are about producing and controlling their own services through centres for independent living, direct payments to enable them to purchase these services for themselves and peer counselling to enable them to develop the necessary skills and support to meet their own self-defined individual and collective needs. This is not an anti-welfare or anti-human services position but one that raises fundamental issues of who is in control and in whose interest?

In looking at the issue of political change, within normalization theory it is difficult to find anything beyond descriptions of the kinds of things devalued people should be entitled to. How to achieve these entitlements at the political level is not really discussed, although Wolfensberger confidently asserts that if we want to valorize someone's social roles:

> we know from social science what the overarching strategies are through which this can be accomplished if that is what one wants to pursue. (Wolfensberger, 1994, p. 96)

I don't know what social science he is referring to, but I have to say that I know very few social scientists who are, any longer, convinced that the concept of social roles has very much value to the development of social theory let alone for the promotion of political action. Not only are Talcott Parsons and Erving Goffman dead in a material sense, but their products are too; the macro and micro versions of role theory.

One can only assume from normalization writings that political change will be a gift from the powerful to the powerless once they have come to a true understanding of disability through exposure to the teachings of normalization and social role valorization. Nowhere does normalization acknowledge that:

> the conviction that one's group is worth fighting for has to come at least partly from within. The alternative is to wait passively for the advantaged group to

confer limited equality which does not essentially alter the status quo, and which it may be motivated to avoid. (Dalley, 1992, p. 128)

Again, materialist theory is much more upfront about political change. It will only be achieved through struggle, and that struggle will be by oppressed groups themselves against the forces that oppress them. In order to do this it is necessary for oppressed groups to organize collectively to confront this oppression. That inevitably means confrontation and conflict with powerful groups, interests and structures, for there are few examples in human history of people willingly giving up power to others.

As far as disabled people are concerned, we have seen over the past fifteen years disabled people coming together to organize themselves as a movement at local, national and international levels. In Britain, for example, in order to harness this growing consciousness of disabled people, to provide a platform to articulate the redefinition of the problem of disability and to give a focus to the campaigns for independent living and against discrimination, the British Council of Organizations of Disabled People (BCODP) was formed in 1981 and its success in the subsequent decade is entirely an achievement of disabled people themselves (Hasler, 1993).

Its conception and subsequent development have been achieved without extensive financial support from government or from traditional organizations for disabled people. On the contrary, BCODP was criticized from the start as being elitist, isolationist, unrepresentative and Marxist by a collection of unrepresentative people with abilities, right- and left-wing academics, isolated and elitist staff and management of traditional organizations and many professionals whose very careers were bound up with keeping disabled people dependent.

Yet despite these attacks, BCODP has gone from strength to strength, now representing over ninety organizations of disabled people and 300,000 disabled individuals. These initiatives not only established BCODP as the only representative voice of disabled people in Britain, but also, by its very success, it stimulated an ever-growing number of disabled people to adopt a disabled identity. Similar stories of the rise of the disabled people's movement could be told from other parts of both the developing and the developed world.

With this growing sense of a collective, political identity has developed the self-confidence not simply to ask for the necessary changes but to demand them and to use a whole range of tactics, including direct action and civil disobedience. What's more, this movement is democratic and accountable to disabled people them-selves (Dreidger, 1988; Oliver, 1990; Davis, 1993) and its collective voice is demanding that we be included in our societies everywhere by ending the oppression that confronts us, not by offering us and our oppressors normalization or social role valorization programmes.

Conclusion

In this paper I have argued that normalization as a social theory is inadequate in that it does not describe experience satisfactorily, its explanation of why disabled people have the kinds of experiences they do is wholly inadequate and its potential for transforming those experi-ences to something better is limited. It is not only those unsympathetic to normalization who question its future, however:

> What does normalization now have to do in order to be a positive force for change in the 1990s. The answer may lie in going back to its roots and realigning itself in relation to other sociological theories. (Brown and Smith, 1992, p. 176)

Whether such a realignment, even with materialist theory, is likely to resuscitate normalization is itself doubtful, because what is at stake is a vision of the kind of society we would like to live in. Normaliza-tion theory offers disabled people the opportunity to be given valued social roles in an unequal society, which values some roles more than others. Materialist social theory offers disabled people the opportunity to transform their own lives and in so doing to transform the society in which they live into one in which all roles are valued. As a disabled person I know which of those choices I prefer and I also know which most of the disabled people I meet prefer.

7

The Relevance of Emancipatory Research for Policy Development

When I started my academic career I believed that social research was the most appropriate way to investigate the social world. It was only a matter of formulating the right questions, using the correct methods to find the answers and reporting the findings in an unbiased and objective manner. Then, so I thought, the world would change for the better. Every stone in the road (to borrow the term from Mary Chapin Carpenter) of my career as an academic researcher took me further away from that view, however. It was not so much a growing disillusionment with the potential and achievements of social research but rather a growing belief that there must be a better way to investigate the social world and to make significant changes for the better. I still retain some elements of that belief in the potential of social research, though its recent track record still leaves considerable room for improvement.

The first stone I encountered in my career as a social researcher was the response I got to my PhD. Of course, there were the usual congratulations from colleagues, friends and relatives, but I don't think any of them ever read it except for my supervisor and my examiners. One colleague, Jan Pahl, was very complimentary about a subsequent paper based upon it that was published in a leading sociology journal and I shall always be grateful for that but, as far as I know, no one ever read it. Bowed but not yet bloodied by this experience I collaborated with John Silver, my consultant in spinal injuries, and we obtained external funding to study the long-term experiences of people with spinal injuries. Hopefully, we asked the right questions, used the correct methods and wrote up the report, which we then turned into a book. But the experiences of people with spinal injuries did not change significantly for all these activities.

As a disabled person and a career(ist) researcher, I was becoming painfully aware that there were significant differences emerging between disabled people and social researchers. This awareness crystallized in a chance meeting I had with David Prior, who had been a PhD student at the same time as me and was now working as a researcher in a social services department. In 1987 we helped to organize a conference in London on behalf of the British Council of Disabled People and the Social Services Research Group to share our concerns with each other. Although this was a very constructive conference, neither organization was well resourced and nothing much happened subsequently. However, it did raise my awareness that the relationship between those who undertake research and those on whom research is undertaken was problematic, not just for disability research, but in a wide range of other areas as well.

The next stone in my road as a social researcher was an invitation to become a member of the Disability Advisory Group of the Joseph Rowntree Foundation. Under the able direction of Janet Lewis and Linda Ward, the group was committed to involving users at all stages of their research and producing findings with direct relevance to policy and social change. Over the next few years many worthwhile projects were funded, including a seminar series organized by Len Barton and myself building upon many of the issues raised at the 1987 conference and aimed at putting disabled people and researchers together for an extended period to hammer out a common agenda. These seminars culminated in a national conference and a special edition of the journal *Disability and Society*. While the conference was well attended, many of the workshops ended in heated arguments and, although many differences were identified, no common agenda emerged. The special edition, however, has been widely read and was very influential in stimulating subsequent debates about disability research.

Since then there have been other stones in my road as a researcher and I have written extensively about them elsewhere, so I don't propose to discuss them here. The final stone in my road as a researcher came when I was invited to give a keynote address at a conference in Dublin organized by the Irish National Disability Authority and the Centre for Disability Studies, University College Dublin, in 2003. It is this paper that I reproduce below. The most recent stone in the road for other disability researchers came when, in 2006, the government invited researchers to tender for a major study on disability. The published protocol used the language and ideas of emancipatory disability research, but whether the research it produces will be truly emancipatory remains to be seen.

~~~~~~~~~~

Using emancipatory methodologies in disability research

Introduction

In this paper I will attempt to provide an historical and contemporary framework for discussions about the development of emancipatory research. I will then look at the main ways in which emancipatory strategies have been developed, notably those using participatory and experiential approaches, before considering the problems that they generate. I will then attempt to locate these in discussions of policy-related research before, finally, proposing an alternative framework that moves beyond methodological individualism and investigatory foundationalism.

Historical and contemporary framework

In looking at the history of research on disability, it is easy to see how it mirrors the history of social research more generally. Previously (Oliver, 1992) I have argued that research has essentially failed disabled people on at least three counts. First, it has failed to accurately capture and reflect the experience of disability from the perspective of disabled people themselves. Second, it has failed to provide information that has been useful to the policy-making process and has contributed little to improving the material conditions under which disabled people live. Third, it has failed to acknowledge the struggles of disabled people themselves and to recognize that disability is not simply a medical or welfare issue, but a political one as well. This situation is summarized in Figure 7.1.

The result of this situation is that many disabled people have become alienated from both the process and product of social research. In this I would suggest that they are not alone. In recent years other minority or oppressed groups – women, black people, the poor, gay men and lesbians and people from other parts of the world – have

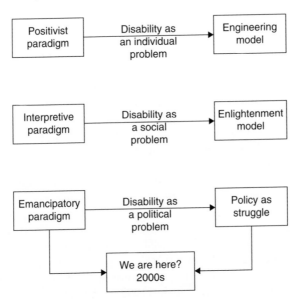

Figure 7.1   A brief history of social research

all voiced similar criticisms in one way or another. While this situation has been recognized in some parts of academia and by some researchers, it remains true that governments and funding bodies still require research to be churned out in the old disabling ways. From the fetishism on methodology that still haunts the Economic and Social Research Council (ESRC) to government obsession with scientific validity, the positivistic approach to social research continues to dominate its funding. However, there have been some attempts to develop emancipatory methodologies and it is to these that I now turn (Oliver, 1997).

Experiential and participatory accounts

The first of these prioritizes and privileges individual experience above ethics, methodology, objectivity and even sometimes the funding body. While I have considerable sympathy with this approach, one problem is that it often assumes that providing faithful accounts of individual experience is enough. Of course, it never is, as many Chicago interactionists, medical sociologists and standpoint feminists could testify if they had been critically reflexive of their own work.

Another problem is a methodological one: the researching of collective as opposed to individual experience. Most of the research techniques involve one researcher and one research subject interacting with one another, the nature of the interaction being shaped by the research paradigm within which the researcher is operating. Even ethnographic approaches to collective phenomena like cultures or subcultures are still dependent upon one-to-one interactions with key informants. After nearly 200 years of social research we still do not have the faintest idea of how to produce collective accounts of collective experience.

A third problem is that the approach can be an exclusionary one which results in noses being bitten off spited faces because it focuses on a false problem: who is entitled to research experience? This debate about who can and should research experience is usually conducted as if it is the first time the issue has ever been raised and with such high emotions that friends as well as enemies often end up being excluded. The final problem is that this approach often fails to tie itself to emancipatory theory or praxis, assuming standpoint epistemology is all that is necessary. As Denzin (1997, p. 54) puts it, 'A politics of action or praxis, however, is seldom offered.'

The second approach calls for participatory strategies involving research subjects. It attempts to deal with the problem of emancipation by sharing or attempting to share responsibility, and indeed blame, with the research participants. The worst exemplar of this is the attempt to do participation by employing a few disabled people as researchers, often without much support or understanding of what that means. Next worse comes involving disability organizations (often non-representative ones) in the process of research production. Least worst involves commitment to involving organizations of disabled people at all stages in the research process, short of overall control over resources and agendas.

The problem with all of these is that they do not confront the objective structures of oppression and, despite personal intentions in many cases, disabled people are still positioned in oppressive ways. Whether we like it or not, failing to give disabled people, through their own representative organizations, complete control over research resources and agendas inevitably positions disabled people as inferior to those who are in control. To preview what I am coming on to say, we create a situation where disabled people are made inferior by our actions, regardless of our intentions.

When we set up research programmes, persuade our organizations to take a specific interest in disability issues and bid into funded initiatives (and I have done all these things myself), we are instrumental in the production of a particular set of social relations. In settling my final accounts with myself, I can no longer pretend that adopting any of the above strategies are the best we can do in current circumstances or that its better than doing nothing. Because of the oppressive structures in which we are located, such actions inevitably keep that oppression in place.

The politics of policy-related research

Certainly the most comprehensive and expensive attempt to provide a universal framework for undertaking disability research has been the work done by the World Health Organization (WHO) to produce a classification system which became the *International Classification of Impairments, Disabilities and Handicaps* (ICIDH) (Wood, 1980). However, since its inception it has been widely criticized as being unusable, confused, confusing and even disablist. Partly as a result of criticisms like these and partly because disability organizations, notably the DPI have forced the issue, the WHO has recently commissioned a review of its scheme and this has now been completed. In the Introduction to ICIDH-2 it claims:

> ICIDH-2 has moved away from a 'consequence of disease' classification (1980 version) to a 'components of health' classification. 'Components of health' defines what constitutes health, whereas 'consequences' focus on the impacts of diseases or other health conditions that may follow as a result. In this way, ICIDH-2 takes a neutral stand with regard to etiology and allows researchers to arrive at causal inferences using appropriate scientific methods. Similarly, this approach is also different from 'determinants' of health or 'risk factors'. To allow for the study of determinants or risk factors, ICIDH-2 encompasses a list of environmental factors that describes the context in which individuals live. (http://www.who.int/icidh/intro.htm)

It is clear from the passage that the authors of the new scheme are distancing themselves from the issue of causality by leaving it open to researchers and, by adding the fourth, environmental component, they are seeking to remedy some of the weaknesses of the earlier scheme. Additionally, by shifting the focus away from disease and onto health, they have tidied up some of the disablist and disabling language that appeared in the original. They also claim elsewhere that the scheme is based upon universalism in order to facilitate the development of universal policy. 'Universal, disability policy, in other words, merely expands the range of human normality to more realistically include empirically grounded human normality' (Bickenbach *et al.*, 1999, p. 1183). But, of course, empirically grounded human normality is code for biologically and medically based classification systems at just the point when social theory is attempting to come to terms with the universality of difference rather than the universality of expanded categories of normality.

What is at stake here is not just social theory but the usefulness or otherwise of ICIDH-2 as tool to facilitate the development of social policy, universal or not, in order to improve the lives of disabled people all over the world. There are a number of different opinions on this matter. Bury (2000), who was involved in the development of the original scheme, argues that much of the criticism of it was unfounded. While he welcomes ICIDH-2, he does suggest that attempts to use positive rather than negative terminology may make it more difficult to identify and tackle the very real disadvantages that disabled people face. On the other hand, Pfeiffer (2000) remains a trenchant critic of all such schemes and argues that the very existence of disabled people is at stake:

> As long as the white, able-bodied, middle-class, Western, male values govern the discussion of public policy, the ICIDH and similar schemes will be used to support them. And in the presence of these values the disability community worldwide faces extinction. Simply revising the details is not sufficient. (Pfeiffer, 2000, p. 1082)

Hurst (2000) takes a middle way between the two positions. While she points to many flaws that remain in ICIDH-2, she suggests that:

> The environmental context covers all areas of life and experience, including attitudes and belief systems, the natural world, services, legislation and policy. If used properly and disabled people are involved in the classification, these factors will build up a considerable body of evidence for major social to change to ensure the inclusion of disabled people. (Hurst, 2000, p. 1086)

She makes the point that any classification scheme is only as good as the way it is used and that disabled people must be fully involved in its utilization.

However, for me, the new scheme has failed to shake off the shackles of 'methodological individualism', which underpins almost all medical and social research, and so its usefulness remains doubtful. Additionally such research is based upon what I shall call 'investigatory foundationalism'; an approach that assumes that there is a real world out there independent of our conceptions of it, which we can, indeed, investigate. As we move into a different kind of world we need a different kind of research enterprise to enable us to understand it and it is to this that I shall now turn.

An alternative framework

No matter what the new scheme may say, the medical and social research enterprises will continue to be based upon methodological individualism underpinned by an investigatory foundationalism. The best definition of the former remains the one provided by Lukes:

> Methodological individualism is a doctrine about explanation which asserts that all attempts to explain social (or individual) phenomena are to be rejected (or, according to a current, more sophisticated version, rejected as 'rock-bottom' explanations) unless they are couched wholly in terms of facts about individuals. (Lukes, 1974a, p. 110)

He goes on, 'Methodological individualism is thus an exclusivist, prescriptive doctrine about what explanations are to look like ... it excludes explanations which appeal to social forces, structural features of society, institutional factors and so on' (Lukes, 1974, p. 122).

Foundationalism is a term used by Hammersley (2000) in his recent defence of objective social research undertaken by the academy. He suggests, 'In its most extreme form, foundationalism presents research, when it is properly executed, as producing conclusions whose validity follows automatically from the "givenness" of the data on which they are based' (Hammersley, 2000, p. 154). While he claims to be distancing himself from such an extreme position, it remains true that almost all social research continues to proceed on the foundational assumption that there is a real world out there and that by using appropriate methods we can investigate it and hence produce worthwhile and workable knowledge about it (Oliver, 2001).

Hence the ICIDH-2 will continue to be used to count, classify and control disabled people all over the world rather than to ensure their emancipation because it remains based upon the twin pillars of methodological individualism and investigatory foundationalism. Hurst, however, has recently suggested that disabled people can prevent this from happening. 'Perceptions will not change without our input. We must influence people to understand that the ICF, if properly used, supports the rights model of disability and will help us collect the evidence to show what our lives are really like' (Hurst, 2000, p. 11).

There are a number of problems with this position, of course. To begin with, the evidence that the vast majority of disabled people throughout the world live deplorable lives (Despouy, 1991) already exists and Hurst's own organization, Disability Awareness in Action, has been in the forefront of drawing international attention to this. Additionally, it is by no means certain that the WHO will continue to involve disabled people now the scheme has been revised. It may return to type and regard its operationalization as a matter of science not politics, as an issue for experts, not 'disabled people'. Further, there is no guaranteee that the international disabled people's movement will see continued involvement with the WHO and ICIDH-2 as high on its list of priorities. Finally, the history of social research in general and disability research in particular is not notable for its success in resolving the problems it has investigated.

Changing the social relations of research production

There are no simple or magic-bullet solutions, however, and even some of the suggestions from oppressed groups themselves border on the naive, for example, standpoint theorists who suggest that all that is needed is for researchers to identify with their research subjects in order to produce accurate accounts of experience. The harder version of this position goes further and argues that shared experience is essential; in other words only women can research women's experience, black people the black experience, disabled people the disability experience and so on. But as Norman Denzin has recently pointed out:

> The standpoint theorist presumes a privileged but problematic place in her own textuality . . . a romantic, utopian impulse organises this work: the belief that if lived experience is recovered, somehow something good will happen in the world. A politics of action or praxis is seldom offered. (Denzin, 1997, p. 54)

My own view is that the crucial issue in developing more useful and less alienating research is that of control, not that of experience. Not all research based on experience accurately reflects that experience and not all 'objective' research fails to accurately capture experience even if the general criticism has some validity. This is not to deny the value of research that gives voice to those previously denied it, but to question whether, by itself, giving voice can ever be enough. If it were, then the work of Mayhew and Engels, let alone Townsend and Abel-Smith, would have resulted in the disappearance of the poor.

If such research is ever to be useful, it must not only faithfully capture the experience of the group being researched, but also be available and accessible to them in their struggles to improve the conditions of their existence. This isn't just about making researchers more accountable but about giving over ultimate control to the research subjects. Elsewhere I have referred to this as the 'changing of the social relations of research production' (Oliver, 1992, p. 101). This does not mean that researchers have to give up researching but that they have to put their knowledge and skills in the hands of research subjects themselves. It also implies that we need to develop a language (or discourse) that does not continue to maintain the artificial distinction between researcher and researched. We do not, as yet, have a language that enables us to talk about research not premised upon the researcher/researched distinction.

Politics and praxis in research

My argument, however, is not intended to replace one naive solution with another – away with experience and on with control, so to speak. The world (of research) is far more complex than that (Oliver, 1997): indeed, it is far more complex than many researchers recognize when they reflect on the relationship between their own politics and their research practice. David Silverman, for example, has recently suggested that researchers can choose one of two roles in relation to their own work; what he calls the scholar or the partisan:

> The partisan is often condemned to ignore features of the world which do not fit his or her preconceived moral or political position. The scholar goes too far in the other direction, wrongly denying that research has any kind of involvement with existing forms of social organisation. Both positions are too extreme and thus fail to cope with the exigencies of the actual relationship between social researchers and society. (Silverman, 1998, p. 93)

It is not simply a matter of researchers choosing whether to adopt partisan or scholarly positions because researchers themselves are not free to make such simple choices. Researchers, I have suggested elsewhere (Oliver, 1997), are trapped between the material and social relations of research production; between the way research is organized and funded and the way it is actually carried out, precisely because the only research that attracts funding is that based upon methodological individualism and investigatory foundationalism.

Research as production

We can only maintain the position that these wider issues are beyond our control if we remain committed to the idea that social research is an act of scientific investigation of the social world. Increasingly, this position is coming under attack from a variety of postmodernist and post-structuralist positions to the point where a view of research as production is becoming increasingly influential. Norman Denzin, in his recent book, puts the moderate version of this position: 'the worlds we study are created, in part, through the texts that we write and perform about them' (Denzin, 1997, p. xiii). In my own research career I am conscious that I have now made that transition from seeing research as an attempt to investigate the world to seeing research as action involved in producing the world. I began the recent study of the disability movement (Campbell and Oliver, 1996) believing that we were investigating the self-organization of disabled people in Britain but I can now only make sense of that experience by seeing it as an act of production, not one of investigation. Once one takes that cognitive leap, not only is research never the same again but also neither is the world itself.

A new epistemology for research praxis is necessary. For me, this epistemology must reject the discourse that sustains investigatory research and replace it with a discourse that suggests that research produces the world. This is not new, of course; Marx argued that the class that owned the means of material production was also responsible for 'mental production' and Gramsci suggested that, under certain conditions, ideas themselves could be material forces. And, finally, Foucault refused to separate knowledge/power, arguing that the structures that maintain one also sustain the other. But, on the whole, research, no matter how radical, committed or emancipatory, has continued to be based upon the investigatory discourse.

As researchers then, we labour to produce ourselves and our worlds. We do not investigate something out there, we do not merely deconstruct and reconstruct discourses about our world. Research as production requires us to engage with the world, not distance ourselves from it, for, ultimately, we are responsible for the product of our labours and as such we must struggle to produce a world in which we can all live as truly human beings. Thus, the research act is not an attempt to change the world through the process of investigation but an attempt to change the world by producing ourselves and others in differing ways from those we have produced before, intentionally or not.

Conclusion

Increasingly, as oppressed groups such as disabled people continue the political process collectively empowering themselves, research practice based upon the investigatory discourse and utilizing 'tourist' approaches by 'tarmac' professors and researchers will find it increasingly difficult to find sites and experiences ripe for colonization. Disabled people and other oppressed groups will no longer be prepared to tolerate exploitative investigatory research based upon exclusionary social relations of research production.

Indeed, one could go further and suggest that the production of all knowledge needs itself to become increasingly a socially distributed process by taking much more seriously the experiential knowledge that oppressed groups produce about themselves and research based upon the discourse of production will have an increasingly important role to play in this. And, who knows, this may eventually lead to the fusion of knowledge and research production into a single coherent activity in which we produce ourselves and our worlds in ways that will make us all truly human.

However, it is clear that disability research continues to remain locked into methodological individualism and investigatory foundationalism, as Hurst points out in respect of the continued classification of disabled people:

> There is no other group of individuals who have been subjected to this analysis of individual characteristics. Women and indigenous people as discreet groups have been analysed, but only in relation to their social, cultural and economic status. An in-depth classification of their individual characteristics has never been seen as necessary as an analysis of their status or for the provision of services or the implementation of policies to implement rights. (Hurst, 2000, p. 1084)

Indeed, any attempt so to do would almost certainly be seen as racist or sexist.

However, I would not like to leave you with the impression that I have abandoned materialism for the cultural and methodological relativity of postmodernism, for, as Oakley correctly points out:

> If there are really no such things as 'facts' about the way people are treated, then there is no such thing as discrimination or oppression. Post-modernism is inherently apolitical. It drives the enforced injustices of social inequality into the personal cupboard of privately experienced suffering. (Oakley, 2000, p. 298)

The real challenge, therefore, for research in the twenty-first century is how to build an enterprise that exposes the real oppression and discrimination that people experience in their everyday lives without merely contributing to the classification and control of marginalized groups who seek nothing more than their full inclusion into the societies in which they live.

8

Disabling or Enabling Welfare: What Next for Disabled People?

The original version of this chapter was written by Colin Barnes and myself as the final chapter in a book on disability and social policy which we wrote in the late 1990s (Barnes and Oliver, 1998). I have included it in this book because it attempts to bring together all of the areas of interest I specified in the Introduction to this new edition; namely theory, policy, practice and personal experience. While I have updated it somewhat, I have resisted the temptation to include any recent specific policy changes within the chapter itself. The reason for this is simply because our original purpose was both to lament the lack of any real vision about what the welfare state would look like from either the left or the right, and to try to tease out such a vision from disabled people's own attempts to reorganize their own welfare through the development and promotion of independent living. A more recent and specific look at the influence of independent living on state-provided welfare can be found in Barnes and Mercer (2006).

While it remains true that since the original chapter was written there have been few attempts to consider what a welfare state in the twenty-first century might look like, the Labour government, in its third term now, claims to have embarked on the most radical reforms in the welfare state since its inception after the Second World War. Whether this programme of reform has concern about increasing expenditure at the heart of it or whether there is a genuine desire to create a welfare state fit for twenty-first century purpose is perhaps an open question. While I do not intend to deal with this in general, at the end of the chapter I do want to return to the issue of what this might mean for disabled people in Britain because many of these reforms directly affecting disabled people do appear to reflect some of the ideas we put forward in the original chapter. In so doing I will bear in mind the old saying, 'Be careful what you wish for because you may just get it.'

~~~~~~~~~~

Disabled people, the welfare state and a welfare society (co-written with Colin Barnes)

Introduction

In this chapter we will suggest that state-sponsored welfare, with particular emphasis on the British experience, has effectively included and excluded disabled people from the mainstream of community life as well as discussing our collective response to this exclusion. We will maintain that, despite the ambiguities and contradictions thrown up by the welfare state, it remains an essential ingredient for the development of a truly inclusionary society. That is to say, a society in which both disabled and non-disabled people can participate and realize their full potential and where the notion of disability and all its associated deprivations are little more than a dim and distant memory.

For us, a vision of how things should and ought to be is fundamental to all social analysis. And this was certainly the driving force underpinning the bulk of the work produced by the key figures associated with the development of the social sciences during the nineteenth and first half of the twentieth centuries. Sadly, it is a feature conspicuous by its absence from so much of what constitutes social theorizing over the last few years, with its quest for the complexities of the meaning of life without much concern with how to change these meanings. Our own view is not dissimilar to that of Marx, who chastised the German idealist philosophers for merely interpreting the world instead of trying to change it.

There are a number of reasons why social theory has distanced itself from political engagement and two significant factors are undoubtedly the rise of the 'new right' in both Britain and America during the early 1980s and the subsequent 'triumph' of capitalism over communism following the collapse of Eastern bloc countries at the end of that particular decade. Since then, with one or two notable exceptions (George and Wilding, 1994; Leonard, 1997), political and academic expediency has prompted many social theorists of social policy to abandon almost completely discussions of and the search for social justice and the 'good society' with a modern welfare state as its centrepiece.

The future of the welfare state

According to John Hills (1995) in his study of the future of welfare for the Joseph Rowntree Foundation, there are three options open to us. First, we can maintain or even improve provision in relation to both need and contemporary living standards, by accepting a slow rise in the share of welfare spending in gross domestic product (GDP) and, hence, in the taxes to pay for it. Second, we can keep welfare spending down by continuing to link benefits to prices and not incomes, although this may not be politically achievable or acceptable, as the poor get poorer. Third, we can maintain the value of certain items but cut out or reduce support for others; this will, of course, mean that priorities will need to be identified and hard choices made.

Not all the political parties find this incremental and reformist approach acceptable. Building on right-wing critiques of the welfare state, David Green suggests that, 'By narrowing opportunities for personal idealism in the service of others, the welfare state has eroded the sense of personal responsibility and mutual obligation on which a resilient civil society rests' (Green, 1993, p. viii). While we would accept that a major problem with state welfare is that it has created dependency rather than allowed for the expression of collective altruism among the population as a whole, mutual obligation under Green's scenario is a euphemism for charity and, therefore, unacceptable to the organized voice of disabled people: the disabled people's movement.

Left-wing critiques also suggest that minor reform of the existing welfare state is not enough. Giddens, for example, provides nothing less than a critique of modernity itself and suggests that the welfare state has failed to adapt to the changing conditions of what he calls the 'post-scarcity society'. This can be done by integrating a wider set of life concerns than those of productivism and thereby developing a politics of second chances. Additionally, a range of social pacts or settlements can be created in the new stakeholder society and all this can be done through 'generative politics as the main means of effectively approaching problems of poverty and social exclusion in the present day' (Giddens, 1994, p. 15).

The problem with this for disabled people, and for other socially excluded groups, as we shall go on to argue later, is that the party political system has hitherto shown itself incapable of representing such a wide disparity of needs and aspirations. This, for us, is important because if social analysis is unable to provide any kind of insight into what such a society should and ought to look like, and of course the policies with which to achieve it, then there is little point in doing it. As Oscar Wilde so cogently pointed out over a century ago in *The Soul of Man Under Socialism* (first published in 1890): 'a map of the world that does not include Utopia is not even worth glancing at . . . Progress is the realisation of utopias' (Wilde, 1966, p. 1090).

In our view, neither of these approaches sees the need to transform rather than reform capitalism and, accordingly, provide only limited visions of what the welfare state might look like under re-energized capitalism (Green) or reformed modernity (Giddens). We shall try to make clear our own vision later in this chapter. For the moment, it is sufficient to point out that, as far as we are concerned, a glimpse of this vision, and an outline of the kind of policies needed to accomplish it, can be found in the writings of disabled people and their organizations. What we now need to consider are the possibilities for change under the middle way or centrist approach of Britain's Labour government.

The limits of possibility or limitless possibilities

One of the first things Margaret Thatcher said when she came to power in 1979 was that disabled people could not expect to be exempt from any necessary changes that were going to be made in the welfare state. Students of recent political history will be struck by the remarkable similarity with a statement made by Tony Blair in his introduction to planned reforms in the welfare state by his Labour government when they took office on 1 May 1997. For us, both of these attempts lack a vision of the possible, for merely tinkering with some bits of the welfare state, notably benefits, are likely to reinforce exclusion rather than facilitate inclusion because at the centre of both statements is the concern to control expenditure on the ever-growing welfare state.

The Thatcherite attempt, based upon the twin strategies of marketization and public expenditure reduction, failed because markets proved no more efficient in allocating resources than professional definitions of need and because benefits, once given, are very hard to take away. It would be a mistake, however, to imagine that history was about to repeat itself, and for two very important reasons. First, Tony Blair was in a stronger position than Margaret Thatcher because Labour always has been broadly supportive of the welfare state, unlike the Tories who always have been either ambivalent to or profoundly anti-welfare. Second, when the Tories came to power, there was no powerful and committed disabled people's movement to defend the interests of disabled people.

So when the Labour government came to power in the late 1990s it sought to increase spending on the welfare state, although it has never attempted to reverse the marketization of welfare; in fact, in some areas it has sought to accelerate it. However, a central concern for the Labour government, like that of the Conservative one before it, has been welfare dependency in general and the rising cost of state benefits, notably incapacity benefit, in particular. Labour's strategy to deal with this is its welfare to work programme; a strategy based on a similar policy introduced by Bill Clinton in the USA.

This certainly could have inclusionary potential because, in our view, it is exclusion from the world of work which is the ultimate cause of the various other exclusions experienced by disabled people (Oliver, 1990; Barnes, 1991). If properly pursued, such an approach will also reduce public expenditure by taking people off social security payments and putting them into work, hence, making more people net givers to, rather than takers from, society. However, Labour's plans to implement this seem to be putting the cart before the horse, namely by cutting benefits before comprehensive strategies for getting people back to work are fully operational.

In our view, such a comprehensive strategy should not be based upon the assumption that all disabled people can work at the same pace as non-disabled people or that everyone with an impairment should work in the conventional sense. As we have said before, expecting severely disabled people to be as productive as non-disabled people is one of the most oppressive aspects of capitalist society (Oliver and Barnes, 1997). This will mean a reappraisal of the very meaning of work, but this is something we must not shy away from. Additionally, there needs to be significant changes in the way work is organized to enable disabled people, and other groups, to participate in it. Finally, there needs to be changes in the way work is allocated which will involve much stronger legal controls on the operation of the labour market rather than continuing the failed policy of voluntarism.

Moreover, the government could go even further than this if it is fully committed to getting disabled people into work. It could, for example, set targets for all government departments and state organizations to achieve in respect of employing disabled people, including organizations such as the health service, local authorities, universities and so on. Additionally, in its dealings with the private sector it could use similar targets to enforce contract compliance. Finally, it could switch the grants it gives to the voluntary sector to organizations controlled and run by disabled people whose record in employing their own puts the traditional voluntary sector to shame.

Such an integrated strategy could, in our view, take hundreds of thousands of disabled people off state welfare payments and, in so doing, reduce the pressures on public expenditure and pave the way for a more equitable and just society. Lest anyone thinks such a strategy is over-simplistic or an impossible dream, it should be remembered that within a few months of the start of the 1939–45 War, 400,000 previously unemployed disabled people were incorporated into Britain's workforce at all levels and made a significant contribution to the war effort (Humphreys and Gordon, 1992).

It must be remembered, however, that the majority of disabled people are over sixty-five and, therefore, such a strategy is largely irrelevant to their needs (Martin, Meltzer and Elliot, 1988). That being said, as far as the nearly 2 million disabled people of working age are concerned, if it is successful, it will succeed in taking many off welfare payments and out of the poverty trap. In turn, this would reduce public expenditure on state benefits, which is precisely what both the government and the overwhelming majority of disabled people want.

Simply cutting cash benefits to disabled people is a strategy doomed to failure for many reasons. To begin with, similar attempts in the past have yielded only marginal savings because disability is a very difficult category to define and hence police. Additionally, cash is not only good for disabled people but also the economy as a whole. For example, Motability, the organization that provides cars for disabled people, buys more cars every year than do car rental firms such as Hertz or Avis, so stimulating the motor industry in particular and the economy as a whole. Finally, all the research evidence we have demonstrates clearly that giving disabled people cash is the best way we know to reduce their dependency on others and the state (Oliver and Zarb, 1992; Zarb and Nadash, 1994).

Also, the problem is not so much that cash benefits create dependency for disabled people, but that vast numbers of people with impairments are socialized into dependency by key components of the traditional welfare state. Special schools, day centres, residential institutions, social security payments that keep people in care all perform this role (Barnes, 1990, 1991) and all could be targeted instead by cash benefits which free people from dependency. Moreover, the vested interests of local authorities who support dependency-creating services, the special schools lobby, the alliance of the charities and the voluntary sector, all of whom are dependent upon disabled people's continued dependence for their very existence, would have to be tackled too. Any government genuinely committed to creating a modern welfare state must ultimately address such services and, of course, the concerns of the vast numbers of people dependent on them for their livelihood.

Let us be clear here that we are not suggesting that the provision of essential services to disabled people should be left to the anarchy of the market or, indeed, to charity, for we know from historical and contemporary analysis that in societies without a state-sponsored welfare system the lives of the vulnerable are greatly impoverished. However, a radical programme that opened up employment opportunities and removed disabling welfare barriers would be something that the disabled people's movement and governments could unite over, although we do not see much hope of this happening in the foreseeable future.

Inclusionary visions for disabled people

As we have already argued, the coming of the welfare state post 1945 has offered the potential for both the inclusion and exclusion of disabled people. In the period following the 1960s, disabled people have increasingly been coming together to collectivize their experiences and, in the process, focus on society's failure to address their needs, and their systematic exclusion from the mainstream of social activity. This has inevitably centred on the welfare state and the way it is organized, as well as looking at the exclusionary practices of society as a whole. At the heart of this analysis lies the call for meaningful and realizable control of the services on which people with impairments are forced to depend, and the introduction of policies capable of creating and sustaining a society whose values and culture will accommodate all its citizens regardless of difference.

What we are proposing is a bottom-up user-led approach to welfare, building upon disabled people's own experiences of the welfare state. Their broadly negative experiences of dependency-creating services have led increasingly large sections of the disabled community to develop their own at both the local and national levels. These include an appropriate range of disability benefits, access and rights to all the necessary information both about impairment and disability, integrated housing schemes, user-led services located in Centres of Integrated Living (CILs) controlled by disabled people, adequately funded personal-assistance schemes, a comprehensive and enforceable anti-discrimination policy applying to all aspects of life and a properly resourced disabled people's movement.

All this is underpinned by a philosophy captured in the demands made by disabled people from all over Europe when they met at a conference in Strasbourg in 1989 to discuss their own struggles for independent living:

> We demand social welfare systems that include assistance services that are consumer controlled and which allow various models of independent living for disabled people, regardless of their disability and income. We demand social welfare legislation which recognises these services as basic civil rights and which provide necessary appeal procedures. (ENIL, 1989)

Elsewhere (Zarb and Oliver, 1993), we have described how all of these elements can be integrated into what we have called the supportive environment model of state-provided welfare, and which we summarize in Figure 8.1.

Furthermore, in an article entitled 'Developing New Services' (1996), Vic Finkelstein and Ossie Stuart outline a similar model to this in two fundamental respects. First, there should be a rigid separation between impairment and disability-based services; what they call medical and lifestyle services (*Ibid.*, p. 187). Second, these services must be provided on an integrated basis; experience shows that attempting to deal with complex issues one at a time is doomed to failure and simply reinforces dependency.

Finkelstein and Stuart (1996) go on to suggest that, as a consequence of their proposals, there will be no place for a National Health Service in their 'brave new world' precisely because it conflates medical and lifestyle needs. We are not convinced of this and, in any case, feel that the precise organizational structure of the revitalized welfare state is not something that can or should be specified in advance. This will emerge as the welfare state is transformed and needs a much broader analysis and debate because such a transformation will involve changes in services for everyone, not just disabled people.

Inclusionary visions for all

It is important to remember here that while impairments of varying kinds, both congenital and acquired, have existed and been recognized throughout recorded history and in all known cultures and societies, social responses to impairments have varied considerably. Disability,

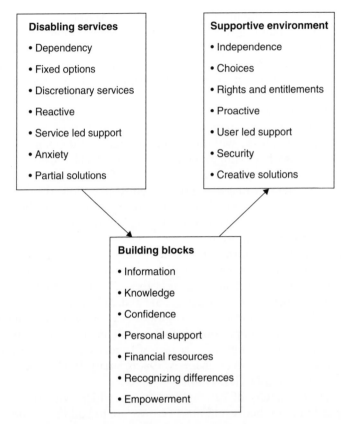

Disabling services

• Dependency

• Fixed options

• Discretionary services

• Reactive

• Service led support

• Anxiety

• Partial solutions

Supportive environment

• Independence

• Choices

• Rights and entitlements

• Proactive

• User led support

• Security

• Creative solutions

Building blocks

• Information

• Knowledge

• Confidence

• Personal support

• Financial resources

• Recognizing differences

• Empowerment

Figure 8.1   Building a supportive environment

or the social oppression of people with perceived impairments, on the other hand, is a social creation. Within western culture, to be a disabled person is to be viewed as, at best, somehow less than whole and, at worst, not quite human. As a consequence, disabled people have and continue to be treated differently from non-disabled peers. Furthermore, from the beginnings of industrialization through to the latter half of the twentieth century this has invariably resulted in their systematic exclusion from the mainstream of community life.

This is not to suggest that disabled people are the only group to experience this form of oppression: patriarchy, classism, racism, heterosexism and ageism have each, to varying degrees, accompanied western economic and cultural development. It is worth remembering too that biological arguments have, historically, been used to justify the differential treatment of women, working-class people, other cultures, minority ethnic groups, lesbians and gay men, children and older people. All of which serves to endorse the fact that the experience of oppression is significantly more complex for anyone who falls within one or more of these categories but just happens to have an accredited impairment.

Furthermore, while a number of important socio-political movements have emerged to represent these groups and, in so doing, work for change, they have, without exception, ignored disability and its impact on those they claim to represent. Several disabled women (Fine and Asch, 1988; Morris, 1991; Wendell, 1996), for example, have drawn attention to the fact that feminism has failed to address the needs of disabled women. As a consequence, traditional assumptions about the problem of disability remained unchallenged until the emergence of the disabled people's movement.

There are two important points to be made about this. To begin with, while we have focused on the oppression of disabled people and the role of the welfare state in both producing and confronting that oppression, similar arguments could and, indeed, have been made about welfare and other oppressed groups (see, for example, Williams, 1989). Additionally, oppression is not a simple matter; people may be oppressed on the grounds of a variety of factors such as impairment, sex, age, sexuality and so on (Morris, 1992b; Stuart, 1992; Shakespeare, Gillespie-Sells and Davies, 1996).

These are matters of central importance which will have to be addressed in both theory and practice if we are to build a welfare state that is inclusive of all and not one that includes some at the expense of others. In theoretical terms, Peter Leonard (1997) suggests that collective resistance to cutbacks in the welfare state might be organized around notions of the 'universal other'. For us, the commonality among different groups is not otherness but the experience of oppression under capitalism. Collective resistance and, indeed, collective reconstruction, must be organized around the different ways that experience manifests itself, and a genuine desire to end our own sectional oppressions by challenging all oppression. The disabled people's movement has made a formidable start in this direction by organizing a collective movement within an oppressed population, which is characterized by difference in terms of impairments and degrees of impairment, gender, class, ethnicity, sexuality and age, but who are united in their opposition to disability: that is the disabling tendencies of modern society (Campbell and Oliver, 1996).

For us it is overwhelmingly obvious that a truly inclusive welfare system must embrace and accommodate the needs of all oppressed individuals and groups. It must not be predicated on false and artificially created distinctions such as those between disabled people and 'carers'. It must include all disabled children, born and unborn, whose right to life and health care must be no more and no less than that of non-disabled peers. It must include children and adults from all backgrounds and diversities of experience. All of which will help to bring about the emergence of an all-embracing culture and value system which values and celebrates the social rather than the selfish, and explores the real meaning of what it is to be human.

In pointing to the issue of being human, we would suggest that the impact of globalization on other cultures and nations has meant that the economic and social forces impacting on welfare are broadly similar all over the world. Questions about the value and affordability of state welfare systems are being asked in all manner of nation states; it is only the context in which these questions are being asked that is different. Thus, in the over-resourced minority world in which we live questions are being asked about cutting existing state welfare structures, whereas in the under-resourced majority world, questions focus on whether such structures should be established in the first place. In our view the right questions are being asked but in the wrong way.

Can we afford to build a world without welfare states?

There is little doubt that in the twenty-first century, if unchecked, capitalist development will have important and potentially negative implications for us all, regardless of which part of the world we live in. After all, capitalism is about the unrelenting search for and the generation of ever-increasing profits. At the bottom line, there are only two ways to produce profit: one is through the exploitation of the environment, and the other is through the exploitation of humans.

The consequences of the mismanagement and unregulated exploitation of the former are becoming increasingly apparent; examples include climatic change, worldwide environmental pollution and an inescapable exhaustion of essential natural resources. Further, the globalization of western values and patterns of consumption is stimulating a demand among the world's population for a lifestyle that cannot be satisfied. As it is a lifestyle dependent upon the continued and unequal distribution of increasingly precious resources (Harrison, 1992; Independent Commission on Population and Quality of Life, 1996) serious environmental, political and social crises will almost certainly ensue. The only way that this situation might be avoided is by the gradual but systematic rejection of the market-led strategies of the past and the generation of a culture that places the needs of the many on a par with those of the few; a culture that celebrates rather than denigrates the meaning of social welfare and, of course, the state's role in the provision of that welfare.

Yet there is a growing consensus among both politicians and policy-makers and the population as a whole that the traditional approach to welfare provision is both economically and politically untenable. There is mounting evidence from a variety of sources from all over the world that conventional top-down professionally led services are counter-productive both in terms of resources, financial and human, and the alleviation of poverty, dependence and suffering (Hellander *et al.*, 1989; Hellander, 1993; Coleridge, 1993; Craig and Mayo, 1995; DS, 1996; Taylor, 1996). We would suggest that the disabled people's movement, against all the odds, has provided a political, cultural and practical foundation on which such a project might be constructed.

Conclusions

Although versions of the good society vary, for us, it is a world in which all human beings, regardless of impairment, age, gender, social class or minority ethnic status, can coexist as equal members of the community, secure in the knowledge that their needs will be met and that their views will be recognized, respected and valued. It will be a very different world from the one in which we now live. It will be a world that is truly democratic, characterized by genuine and meaningful equality of opportunity, with far greater equity in terms of wealth and income, with enhanced choice and freedom, and with a proper regard for environmental and social continuity. The creation of such a world will be a long and difficult process.

But without a vision of how things should and ought to be it is easy to lose your way and give up in the face of adversity and opposition. As we move into the twenty-first century, there is a growing sense of impotence among both politicians and academics. Politicians feel unable to control globalized economic forces and academics, obsessed with the collapse of modernity and the coming of postmodernity, no longer attempt to describe the world as it ought to be.

In our view, disabled people and their organizations have taken the first steps and initiated a glimpse of that vision of how the world ought to be. In fact, for us, disabled people have no choice but to attempt to build a better world because it is impossible to have a vision of inclusionary capitalism; instead we need a world where impairment is valued and celebrated and all disabling barriers are eradicated. Such a world would be inclusionary for all and it is up to everyone, but especially those involved in the development and implementation of social policy – both planners and practitioners – to nurture it and help make it a reality.

Wishing for welfare

(written by Mike Oliver)

There are three main planks to the government's radical programme of welfare reform in respect of disabled people: health, social care and benefits. The language used in official documents reflects the central concerns that disabled people and other groups have used in putting forward their own welfare agendas: rights and entitlements, independence, choice and placing users at the centre of services. While this indicates that government has listened to our concerns, suspicion remains that controlling expenditure is at the heart of the reforms. The rest of this chapter will be my own personal reflections on the possibilities and dangers of these changes for disabled people.

Rights and entitlements have been at the top of the agenda for disabled people for many years now and the Disability Discrimination Act (DDA) (1995) was the government's response to this. Since its passage there have been various changes and amendments and substantive duties imposed on public authorities, as well as private organizations. However, its lack of enforcement has impacted negatively and many fear that the replacement of the Disability Rights Commission (DRC) by the Equality and Human Rights Commission (EHRC) will make matters worse, both because disability may not be the central concern for a single commission and because the EHRC so far seems to prefer the public education rather than legal enforcement approach to discrimination.

This is directly relevant to welfare reforms in the area of discrimination in the workplace. One of the main aims of the reforms is to get at least a million people off incapacity benefit and into work. One way to do this would be to take a much more aggressive enforcement approach to employers who discriminate against disabled people in the labour market, but, instead, the government has decided to change the way entitlement to benefit will be assessed and to replace incapacity benefit with a short-term allowance for those deemed fit to work. They recognize that for many getting a job will be a problem, but they intend to solve this by providing employment support to individuals. Providing individual solutions to structural problems is hardly radical and some would suggest, doomed to failure. In Chapter 10 I discuss an earlier failed attempt to reform welfare by getting people off incapacity benefit.

Central to the social care reforms is the concept of independence. Building on the success of direct payments given to disabled people to buy in their own support, these reforms propose to provide all recipients of social care services with their own individualized budgets which can be used to meet their own support needs. Individuals themselves, or with the support of their families or care managers, can then use these budgets to exercise choice and control over how their support needs are met. The aim is to build on the success of direct payments but these reforms will require far more radical changes to the organization of social care services than direct payments and for this reason a number of pilot programmes are being rolled out all over the country.

While the government is going ahead with these changes, there are a number of possible problems that may arise. To begin with, the problems of providing services that overlap with health have bedevilled the welfare state from the beginning and, although the plans envisage moving to personal health budgets as well, there appears to be no vision of how these budgets will interface with each other. Additionally, many disabled people and their families rely on a whole range of state benefits and there is no clear idea as to what will happen to them when we all have our own individualized budgets. Already there is concern among some disabled people that their benefits will end up in their budget pots. Finally, it is unclear where charging policies fit in to the new vision, especially in light of current attempts by local authorities under government guidance to restrict access to social care only to those whose needs are substantial or critical.

Whether these reforms will give disabled people what they wish for or leave us more impoverished and excluded remains to be seen. As we pointed out earlier, the welfare state (reformed or not) can be both enabling and disabling. Which it becomes will be played out in the arena of politics not policy and disabled people need a powerful voice to make sure our wishes are met. Whether we have such a voice will be discussed in the next chapter.

9

Disability Politics and the Disabled People's Movement in Britain

A few years ago Colin Barnes and myself were asked to write a discussion paper on what was happening to the disabled people's movement in Britain for *Coalition*, the journal of the Greater Manchester Coalition of Disabled People (GMCDP) (2006). This we did, but it did not generate the kind of debate that *Coalition* had hoped for. Sometime later, I met Vic Finkelstein when we were both in hospital and he told me he had written a detailed response, but that the Manchester Coalition were having difficulties publishing it. He sent us both copies and it was posted on the Disability Archive at the University of Leeds. I also suggested to him that it would be good to include it in the second edition of this book and he agreed.

I am particularly pleased because Vic has played a key role in our understandings of disability and, personally, I have been profoundly influenced by his ideas. I have not always agreed with him nor he with me, as this chapter hopefully will make clear. In our disagreements, I'm sure that I have come round to his way of thinking much more than he has come round to mine. Some ten years ago, at his sixtieth birthday celebrations, I was asked by his daughters Anna and Rebecca to say a few words about him as part of the festivities. The best way I could sum up his contribution was to call him 'the pied piper of the disabled people's movement' because we all dance to his tune. Eventually.

In order for the chapter to read as a dialogue between myself and Vic, I include the original version of the paper that appeared in *Coalition*, before Colin and I amended it prior to publication. In it I argue that the disabled people's movement has lost its way since the middle of the 1990s and highlight the main reasons for this. The second part is Vic's response, where he takes issue with our analysis and suggests a set of different reasons for this loss of direction. He also broadens his analysis somewhat in order to take issue with our interpretation of the social model, as well as our approach to independent living. I have slightly edited Vic's contribution to keep the dialogue. The final part of this chapter is my short response to Vic's contribution; I suggest that he misunderstands my formulation of the social model and I question his unrealistic stance on direct payments as a way of promoting independent living.

Many of the issues that are raised in what follows are taken up again in the final two chapters of this book. One final point needs to be made herein. In our contribution we refer to our collective self-organization as the disabled people's movement because we believe that the term 'disability movement' has been usurped by the big charities and a variety of government quangos. Not only do they steal our ideas but our name as well. In the final chapter, I attempt to rebrand and rename this disabled people's movement as 'disabling corporatism', but only history will judge how successful I have been. Vic, for his own reasons, continues to use the term disability movement. It should also be noted that the British Council of Disabled People (BCODP) has since changed its name to the United Kingdom Council of Disabled People (UKCDP) but I have retained the original title in both contributions.

~~~~~~~~~~

The disabled people's movement: where did it all go wrong?

(written by Mike Oliver and Colin Barnes)

Introduction

In earlier publications (Oliver, 1990; Barnes, 1991) we suggested that the pursuit of a single aim or goal in disability politics would be a mistake, would be bound to lead to a dilution in the collective energy and commitment of disabled people and would ultimately achieve little. Although we used slightly different language, we argued that what has now come to be known as the rights-based approach to disability would be counter-productive if pursued as an end in itself rather than as a means to an end. Having legal rights does not mean that they will be enforced and, even if they are, that enforcement will achieve the desired aims. Narrow legalistic approaches tend to benefit those professionals who work in the rights industry as much if not more than those they are supposed to serve. We further suggested that organizations of disabled people were needed to ensure that such an approach remained accountable to disabled people who, after all, had produced the idea in the first place.

By the middle of the 1990s, we saw the rise of many organizations controlled and run by disabled people at local, national and international levels to the point where we were able to suggest that these organizations constituted *the* disabled people's movement, with the potential to exert a powerful influence on political and social change. In one article we warned that even at the high point of this development the movement faced a number of dilemmas:

> To get too close to the Government is to risk incorporation and end up carrying out their proposals rather than ours. To move too far away is to risk marginalization and eventual demise. To collaborate too eagerly with the organizations for disabled people risks having our agendas taken over by them, and having them presented both to us and to politicians as theirs. To remain aloof risks appearing unrealistic and/or unreasonable, and denies possible access to much needed resources. (Barnes and Oliver, 1995, p. 115)

Here we want to suggest that this caution was justified, and that the drift towards a rights-based approach that now dominates disability politics has compounded the problem. Indeed, since the turn of the millennium we have witnessed the growing professionalization of disability rights and the wilful decimation of organizations controlled and run by disabled people at the local and national level by successive government policies, despite rhetoric to the contrary. As a result, we no longer have a strong and powerful disabled people's movement and the struggle to improve disabled people's life chances has taken a step backwards. In making this argument we are not seeking to apportion blame and make veiled personal attacks, nor exempt ourselves from taking some responsibility as disability activists engaged in much of what has happened. Instead, we hope to provide an analysis of what we think has gone wrong in the hope that we can help reverse the situation.

The rise of the disabled people's movement

We do not have the time or space to discuss the rise of this democratic movement in detail and in any case, it has been adequately covered elsewhere (Campbell and Oliver, 1996). However, it is necessary to chart its origins as this is relevant to our later discussion of where the movement went wrong.

While some disability charities had been in existence throughout the twentieth century, it was not until the 1970s that a significant number of organizations controlled and run by disabled people began to emerge. A key factor in this was undoubtedly the postwar affluence that led one prime minister to tell the British population in the 1960s that 'you've never had it so good'. Disabled people had not experienced the rising living standards of the rest of the population and relied on means-tested benefits and their own families to survive in the community. Those whose families were unable to support them usually ended up in long-stay institutions of one kind or another.

Not only were the long-standing disability charities unable to ensure that those that they purported to support were able to get their share of the increasing affluence that was all around, but also often they were compliant in the continued exclusion of disabled people from society. These charities often provided residential care and other segregated facilities that kept disabled people out of society, but they often colluded with government by arguing that this was the best disabled people could expect and that such provision was for our own good. For this compliance they, of course, received their rewards, which included government contracts and grants, invitations to top-table discussions about the problems of disabled people, all-expenses-paid trips to conferences in exotic parts of the world and personal honours for their services to disabled people.

More and more disabled people were growing increasingly dissatisfied with their continued exclusion from rising living standards and the failure of disability organizations to articulate this at a political level. After unsuccessful attempts to infiltrate and radicalize these disability organizations, some disabled people embarked on ambitious attempts to create and build our own organizations in which non-disabled people would have little or no role to play. Despite hostility from the existing disability organizations and partly inspired by the success of organizations controlled by disabled people in other parts of the world, notably the USA, by the end of the 1970s a small number of these organizations had emerged.

Flushed by the success of this, and angry at the continuing hostility of the disability charities, these organizations came together in 1981 and formed the British Council of Organizations of Disabled People, later to become the British Council of Disabled People (BCODP). As an umbrella organization, BCODP became the springboard for the development of many other organizations at local, national and international level. By the end of the 1980s BCODP had approximately 130 organizations affiliated to it and it was a key member of Disabled Peoples International. Out of all this activity, three big ideas had emerged (Hasler, 1993): the social model of disability; independent living; and rights, in particular the right not to experience discrimination. These ideas were beginning to have an impact on policy and service delivery at both national and local levels, as well as challenging the position of the disability charities whose policies and ideologies were being increasingly seen as outdated, inappropriate and even oppressive.

By the 1990s there was a growing self-confidence among disabled people and those organizations that we controlled. Strong links with a few universities resulted in the emergence of what came to be called disability studies and this gave a legitimacy to the big ideas that had emerged in the previous decade. Disabled people also began to take to the streets when our concerns and wishes were either ignored or derided; notably in support of fully accessible public transport and against disabling media images as portrayed by television programmes such as the telethon. These actions were singularly successful, forcing transport providers to change their policies and the television companies to take the telethon off the air. A loose-knit organization known as the Direct Action Network (DAN) emerged to coordinate these activities and demonstrations began to take place up and down the country in support of a wide variety of issues.

All this forced both government and the disability charities to take notice. Building on its links with disability studies, BCODP produced an authoritative report (Barnes, 1991) based upon the government's own statistics, which demonstrated the extent of discrimination faced by disabled people in Britain. As a consequence, disabled people increasingly took to the streets in righteous anger and both government and the disability charities reversed their previously held positions and conceded that discrimination was a major problem in disabled people's lives. So much so that, in 1995, after many false starts the Disability Discrimination Act became law.

The seeds of destruction

From the preceding analysis it would not be unreasonable to conclude that by the mid-1990s the disabled people's movement had reached the height of its powers and that disabled people were now ready for the final push to claim their full inclusion into society. However, it would be wrong to draw this conclusion because it was precisely at this point that the democratic movement of disabled people began to go into decline. In this section we will attempt to tease out some of the reasons for this.

As we suggested earlier, the disability charities had initially opposed the idea that disabled people should have their rights not to be discriminated against enshrined in law. However, the publication of a report produced by the Committee on Restrictions Against Disabled People (CORAD, 1982) forced them to have a rethink and by the mid-1980s they set up their own think tank, to be called the Voluntary Organizations For Anti-Discrimination Legislation (VOADL). Ironically, BCODP was invited to send a representative to the first meeting, which was held at a venue completely inaccessible to wheelchair users. Despite this, BCODP continued to participate in VOADL meetings but with 'observer status' only. This situation remained when, in the 1990s, VOADL transformed itself into Rights Now as the impetus for anti-discrimination legislation became ever stronger.

After the failure of several parliamentary attempts to get anti-discrimination legislation onto the statute books, Rights Now organized a mass rally in 1994 in Trafalgar Square. Speaker after speaker, both from the disability charities and the democratic disability movement expressed their anger at government's failure to act and demanded proper civil rights legislation. This rally represented a full about face for the disability charities, who not only insisted that disabled people had rights but also attempted to claim this idea as their own, hence attempting to rewrite disability history in the process. The Direct Action Network also kept the pressure on government by targeting particular parliamentary constituencies for mass demonstrations. This was particularly successful at a by-election in Winchester, when a large government majority was overturned as a direct result of disabled people taking to the streets.

All this made the passage of the Disability Discrimination Act (DDA) inevitable and, in 1995, such legislation was duly passed. However, the disabled people's movement had major concerns about it arguing that it was neither comprehensive nor enforceable. Hence, when the government established a task force to oversee its implementation, while BCODP refused to participate, the disability charities fell over themselves to nominate members. Some disabled individuals who had previously occupied leadership roles in the disabled people's movement also chose to get involved, arguing that it was better to be involved and hence able to influence subsequent changes than remain in isolation. This remained the situation when a new government was elected and the task force was disbanded and a Disability Rights Commission (DRC) appointed.

It could be argued that all these developments mean that disability politics had come of age and that the onward march of progress would ensure that disabled people would finally achieve their goal of the full inclusion into society. However, as we have already intimated, we do not share this view. The coming to power of a new government, which appeared to be more willing to listen to the voice of disabled people, was a problem in itself in that a movement that had cut its teeth on oppositional politics had little experience in participatory politics. However, the big charities were only too willing to step in and fill the void. Since the late 1990s, this combination of government and the charities has taken over the big ideas of the disability movement, usurped its language and undertaken further initiatives which promise much and deliver little.

BCODP, which has always been the lead organization of the disabled people's movement, has experienced considerable political isolation, although it has striven to maintain parliamentary links of its own. It has also, along with many other organizations of disabled people, found it difficult to attract core funding, particularly as government was more concerned to support the DRC and its other initiatives, none of which are accountable to disabled people. It has also run into difficulties in seeking to promote the idea of independent living. Initially, it did this through the Independent Living Sub-Committee but this later emerged as a separate organization called the National Centre for Independent Living (NCIL). Not only did this mean that NCIL was no longer directly accountable to disabled people but it also did little to challenge the government's view that independent living and direct payments were the same thing. Perhaps this was because the government was its main funder, although it now appears that this was temporary and NCIL is itself under threat.

The political influence of DAN has also declined. Shortly after New Labour came to power in 1997 it pulled off its most spectacular demonstration of all. The government, with an extremely large majority, was exercising its power by tackling the expensive and seemingly intractable problem concerning the rising cost of incapacity benefit. It was determined to reduce these costs and its aggressive approach provoked anxiety among severely disabled people. DAN targeted Downing Street and a small number of disability activists got as far as the Prime Minister's front door and threw red paint over it, symbolising the blood of disabled people that would be shed if the government plans were passed. This demonstration attracted widespread international attention, as far afield as New Zealand and America, and the plans were quietly dropped. While this was a success for DAN in once sense, it left it with a difficult legacy to follow. As DAN was committed to peaceful direct action it was virtually impossible to organize something bigger or better and, while DAN has continued, its influence has steadily declined. The paradox of failing at the moment of success has been captured in the lyrics of a song: 'There's no success like failure and failure's no success at all' (Bob Dylan).

At the local level there has also been a decline in the number of local coalitions and CILs, as local authorities and government agencies cut their funding and face competition from local branches of the big charities. Despite the Prime Minister's Strategy Unit Report claim that by the year 2010 every locale 'should have a user led organisation modelled on an existing CIL' (PMSU, 2005, p. 67), there is a wealth of evidence from a variety of sources showing that existing CILs are closing down at an alarming rate.

There is another factor in the decline of the disabled people's movement which makes a nonsense of those who have criticized its adherence to a social model that ignores impairment and this is the very real toll that impairment takes on both the leadership and other activists within the movement. Both through untimely deaths and burn-out, the disabled people's movement has been robbed of many important members long before their useful contributions have been completed. Of course, all political movements suffer from this but, we would argue, not to anything like the same extent as the disabled people's movement. Finally, as we have already intimated, some of the leaders of the movement have opted to put upward personal mobility ahead of the needs of the movement itself. We do not criticize personally those who have done this, nor do we exempt ourselves.

Where are we now?

Recently DEMOS, an independent think tank, was commissioned by SCOPE to revisit the original BCODP Report on discrimination with a view to assessing the progress that has been made since then. Overall the report, entitled *Disablist Britain: barriers to Independent Living for Disabled People in 2006*, concludes that, despite all the apparent progress that has been made since the original report was launched, the underlying reality is that disabled people continue to face the same barriers that they have always faced and that 'disablism remains rife throughout Britain' (Gillinson, Huber and Miller, 2006).

So progress over the last ten years has been more apparent than real. Alongside this, we have seen the decline in both the numbers and influence of organizations controlled by disabled people and the commensurate resurrection of the big charities. Additionally, the government has created a number of new non-accountable organizations, including the DRC and the Office of Disability Issues. It has also shown a willingness to recognize and support the big charities as the supposed legitimate voice of disabled people.

In our view this is extremely dangerous for disabled people. Our history has taught us that these organizations in the recent past played a leading role in keeping us oppressed and out of society. Name changes, tidying up the language they use and employing token disabled people cannot disguise the underlying reality that these organizations are primarily interested in themselves and that they will say and do anything that is politically expedient in order for them to retain their influence with government. Perhaps all this would not matter if we could all look forward to a peaceful future in which living standards continually rise and are distributed evenly throughout society.

Indeed, the choices available to disabled activists in the new millennium are different from those that went before. The gradual shift away from institutional to community 'care' over the last thirty years, the accompanying growth of disability benefits, the introduction of the DDA and the Community Care (Direct Payments) Act and the establishment of government-sponsored 'disability' bodies such as the DRC and the Office of Disability Issues (ODI), and the effective rebranding of disability politics as a rights issue promotes the illusion of equality and inclusion. Although the reality is quite different, these developments will make it much more difficult to generate a new and revitalized disabled people's movement to fight for meaningful change. Whether a third generation of disability activists can rise to this challenge remains to be seen. We sincerely hope so as the current situation does not bode well for the future of disabled people.

Conclusion

A recent paper (Lee, 2002) has suggested that we have been guilty of promoting a romanticized view of the relationship between disability and politics and that there are very real gains to be had by using the traditional political system and joining coalitions with the big charities. As we have tried to make clear in this paper, we are not sure what progress has been made by this politics of coalition and, equally importantly, we have tried to point out the real dangers of relying on the big charities to speak for us.

So far, we have tried to better understand the issues facing disabled people in twenty-first-century Britain. Clearly, we were over-optimistic about the role of new social movements in producing significant social change. Many of the movements operating in the last century have either been incorporated into government or become marginal to the political process. Regrettably, we would suggest, this has become the temporary fate of the disabled people's movement. Most significantly, there has been no coming together of the disabled people's movement and other political groups, such as the lesbian and gay movement, for example, to create more powerful alliances. And, in some respects, the social divisions that characterized British society in the twentieth century, such as ethnicity, race and religion, for instance, have widened.

Most importantly, the prohibition of racism by law has done little to eliminate these problems. By the same token, the singular focus on disability as a rights issue will not solve the problem of disability discrimination and oppression. At best, it will benefit only a very small minority of the disabled population: those with plenty of money to spend and those employed in the legal and related professions. At worst, it will legitimize further the rhetoric of those who support an inherently unjust and inequitable society and hamper further the struggle for meaningful equality and justice.

We still believe that the only viable long-term political strategy for disabled people is to be part of a far wider struggle to create a better society for all. It is a struggle that must take on board the fact that twenty-first-century Britain is a society near the top of world league tables for illiteracy, teenage pregnancy, childhood obesity, school exclusions and relative poverty. All of this must be contextualized within a global society characterized by an exploding human population, growing cultural conflict, climatic change and environmental degradation. These are the issues that today's generation will almost certainly have to address if the struggle for a society fit for all is to be achieved.

The 'social model of disability' and the disability movement

(written by Vic Finkelstein)

In their August 2006 *Coalition* article, Mike Oliver and Colin Barnes argue that 'pursuit of a single aim or goal in disability politics would be a mistake'. If it is *this* mistake that is held to account for the disability movement's current problems then I can't agree. Such a view, I think, is too narrow. It seems to me that there *are* times when a single aim ought to be pursued, times when several aims need to be followed simultaneously, and even times when we may need to withdraw from public action and take *time out* to explore ideas about multiple aims (this is what the Union of the Physically Impaired Against Segregation [UPIAS] did when it responded to the failure of the Disablement Income Group [DIG] and withdrew to conduct an internal discussion about a new way of interpreting the problems that we face).

On the other hand, they go on to add, 'Although we used slightly different language we argued that what has now come to be known as the rights-based approach to disability would be counter-productive if pursued as an end in itself rather than as a means to an end.' In *this* case I do agree. Pursuing 'the rights-based approach ... as an end in itself' would mean an exclusive redirection of the disability movement's limited energy onto parliamentary lobbying, leaving no time for grass-roots development. However, I know of no advocate of the rights-based approach who would maintain it was the *only* course of action that they followed. Replying to my 1996 *Disability Now* article criticizing the direction of the disability movement, for example, Jane Campbell wrote to me mentioning a string of activities BCODP pursued *at the same time* as campaigning for rights.

I think the actual concern when an emancipatory movement's survival is threatened should not just be about aims or goals but, first, whether the movement has lost, did not use, or does not have, a tool that enables insight into the aim or goal that *does* provide an effective way forward. The 'social model of disability' functioned as such a tool for the UK disability movement. As I see it, the important questions then become: 'didn't the movement's leadership use, or didn't they really understand the social model of disability?'

Disability models

In 1996 I wrote a paper on different disability models (Finkelstein, 1996b). I wrote this at the time because I had become increasingly concerned about the way people were misunderstanding what 'models' are and, more specifically the UPIAS radical interpretation of 'disability' that Mike Oliver had developed as the 'social model of disability'. I wanted to show that social models only really make sense when understood in particular contexts. Change the context and the model may well become inappropriate. I tried to illustrate a whole range of models – all associated with 'disability' but all very different.

For example, this is what I mean: a model house for a child living in a very hot climate would be very different if it were modelled for a child living in a very cold climate. The former might depict a light post-and-canvas construction and the latter a more robust solid brick construction. They look very different but both could be labelled as 'model houses'. The models enable different insights in the different versions. The point is: (a) if a model is too generalized it covers everything and becomes useless as a 'model' and (b) a model may retain its name even when it has become something notably different because the context (e.g. the 'society') has radically changed.

In 1976, I wrote in the UPIAS *Fundamental Principles of Disability* document, 'it is society which disables physically impaired people. *Disability* is something imposed on top of our impairments'. In this interpretation it is obvious and clear that if society changes, or there are significant changes in society, then the disability model can also change. Major upheavals in the world and UK in the 1990s (cheered on by the new Blatcherite Labour Party's privatization programme for the health and social services) need to be understood as changing the social context for models of disability. These social changes were unleashed by, for example, the miners' strike defeat in 1985, the Soviet Union collapse 1991 and the Labour Party's constitutional change – abandoning a socialist platform in 1995 – and, later, its election in 1997.

In concert with these global changes in society, I believe that it was no accident that social models started to change. It was in this decade that the politically centre right in the disability movement became more strident in asserting its demand that the social model of disability had to change! In 1992 Liz Crow launched the attack in her paper 'Renewing the Social Model of Disability' (Crow, 1992). This was followed by Tom Shakespeare (1993) with a robust attack demanding that the social model of disability must be 'rectified'. By the year 2000 the 'rectifiers' were secure enough to state:

> We need to produce an updated social model of disability that; includes a positive statement about us; recognises our diversity and difference; recognises institutionalised discrimination; talks about choice; recognises that not all the things that exclude us are about society's barriers; and talks about barriers (attitudes and access). (GLAD, 2000)

This statement is generalized enough to cover all human social behaviour and is quite useless as a 'disability' model – a real 'shopping

basket' approach which enables people to pick and choose any interpretation that happens to suit their personal ambitions; and it perfectly
matches the privatization programme of New Labour for a free market
in health and social services.

Rights

It was in the 1990s, too, that alongside the attack   ining
the social model of disability the BCODP turned it   from
grass-roots work to parliamentary lobbying and made   mpaign
for comprehensive anti-discrimination its top priorit   ding to
Richard Wood, then its chief executive (1996). Qu   ly, if all
major political parties are now in favour of a free m   sort out
problems in the health and social services rather th   ng better
ways for users to exercise democratic control over thes   ices upon
which they depend, then many disabled people will conclude that they
have no choice other than to suck up to parliament in the hope that
we will not be forgotten. With never enough personal income to buy
in services, or merit attention from significant sectors of the market
to solicit our custom, all we can do is beg that our human 'rights' are
recognized and policed. The changes of the 1990s, then, led to the
emergence of meaningless social models of disability coupled with a
shifting focus onto 'social rights'. Thereafter it was only the next simple
step to interpret the social model of disability as a 'rights' model.

   For me, then, 1996 was the crunch year. At this time I never saw,
and cannot recall, any robust criticism of what was happening in the
disability movement. This was when I made my concerns public. Having previously been prevented from speaking at a BCODP Council
meeting (when Dick Leaman and I travelled to Derbyshire to speak
at a BCODP meeting about our worries regarding developments in
the movement), my concerns became so strong that I sent a paper
to *Disability Now* for publication! The full version was published in
Coalition:

> The adoption of Anti-Discrimination Legislation (ADL) is about to drive a
> wedge through the heart of the disabled community as the artificial alliance
> promoting ADL predictably falls apart. The disability movement with its
> adoption of pressure group politics campaigning for this legislation not only
> followed all the mistakes of yesterday's DIG but is threatening to end up the
> same way, having started full of enthusiasm and ending up as, in the words of the
> DAIL Magazine editorial [referring to their AGM meeting], 'a disappointing
> affair'. (Finkelstein, 1996c)

Apart from Anne Rae's support, my views were met in public by – 'silence' – and the unified core of the disability movement merrily continued its political journey into fragmentation. It gives me no pleasure in seeing this foreboding anticipation realized. In 2001 I tried again and in my presentation to the Greater Manchester Coalition of Disabled People September open meeting I said:

> Civil Rights are about individual people or groups of people – this is a legalistic approach to emancipation. ... the campaign for 'disability rights' does not depend on, nor is it a reflection of, the social model [or, to avoid confusion, the radical UPIAS *interpretation*] of disability. (Finkelstein, 2002, p. 14)

In the 'rights' approach, parliament grants legal rights to those it *defines* as 'disabled'. The focus is on identifying characteristics of the individual, rather than the nature of society, and then making selected 'concessions' to those so defined. I then added:

> It's not just that the liberal right wants to inherit the ideological underpinnings of the social model of disability, but they want also to rewrite (reclaim) the past. The left may lose this battle, but at least let's be clear about what is being done to the social model of disability. (Finkelstein, 2002, p. 14.)

Further on in this paper I wrote: 'what happens to disabled people is an integral part of the way our society is organised and structured ... I believe that we cannot understand or deal with disability without dealing with the essential nature of society itself' (Finkelstein, 2002, p. 14).

One underlying theme has remained the same throughout all my writing on 'disability' since I came to the UK – 'disability' should be understood and addressed as a social (i.e., comprehensive) and not as a personal (i.e., individual) phenomenon. Even when a single approach is emphasized for a given period, the UPIAS 'interpretation' of disability (and logically the 'radical' social model of disability) makes no sense if *one* component (or attribute) is selected as providing the *only* route to emancipation. The 'radical' social model of disability provides an overarching view of disability and cannot be placed alongside selected elements as if they were of equal value.

The troika

In the 1990s Mike Oliver's view, on the other hand, was and has remained, that the 'social model of disability' and 'civil rights', alongside with 'independent living' are harmonious components in our struggle for emancipation. 'In the last 30 years we have begun to shake off the dead hand of charity ... In so doing we have built a political and social movement that does offer us the very real possibility of "changing our futures"' (Campbell and Oliver, 1996). Mike maintains that these advances were founded on three *big ideas*: 'the social model of disability, independent living and civil rights' (Oliver, 1996b).

I don't agree. I don't see how 'components' of a model can be given equal value to the model itself! This is like suggesting, in my model house analogy, that we can say 'we have built a new house founded on three big ideas: the model (of the house), doors (a component, attribute, or element of a house) and a roof (another component of a house)'. Not only are the 'door' and 'roof' components of the overarching house 'model', but also there is no particular reason to select these components rather than other attributes (such as 'windows' and 'floors') to put alongside the overarching 'model'. You could just as well replace the components 'independent living and civil rights' in your 'three big ideas' with 'disability culture' and 'direct payments' (perhaps even making a better case!): but you can't remove or replace the social model of disability 'big idea' without undermining the modern UK disability movement's political and social history.

My point is that 'independent living', 'civil rights', 'disability culture' and 'direct payments', etc., are *internal components*, or elements, of the 'social model of disability'. *In other words these are 'insights' that are revealed by exploring the model!* If we believe that over-emphasizing a component of the model 'would be counter-productive if pursued as an end in itself rather than as a means to an end (as Mike Oliver and Colin Barnes argue) then we are interpreting current problems in the disability movement from an 'inside out' (*internal*) rather than an 'outside in' viewpoint: 'the pursuit of a single aim or goal in disability politics would be a mistake'.

Inside out?

The result is that Mike and Colin do not offer a *single* interpretation of what happened in the 1990s structure of society, 'outside' there, which facilitated the rising dominance of the 'rights-based approach' in the disability movement, 'inside' here. Far from making a credible criticism of the disability movement's misleading over-emphasis on 'civil rights', they adopt the same 'inside-out' approach in their analysis! This is not helped at all by their studious avoidance of naming anyone whose views may be identified, read, analyzed and praised or criticized for leading or influencing the movement into its present situation. Both Mike and Colin, after all, were in the forefront championing civil rights.

It's only in the last paragraph that Mike and Colin put forward a comprehensive social (socialist?) connection with the disability movement's emancipatory struggle:

> We still believe that the only viable long-term political strategy for disabled people is to be part of a far wider struggle to create a better society for all. It is a struggle that must take on board the fact that twenty–first-century Britain is a society near the top of world league tables for illiteracy, teenage pregnancy, childhood obesity, school exclusions and relative poverty. All of this must be contextualized within a global society characterized by an exploding human population, growing cultural conflict, climatic change and environmental degradation. These are the issues that today's generation will almost certainly have to address if the struggle for a society fit for all is to be achieved. (See p. 142 above)

However, it's all very well saying that we need 'to be part of a far wider struggle to create a better society for all', but these remain empty words when unbacked with any suggestion of how and what the disability movement ought to do. And why pass on responsibility to 'today's generation' for addressing the 'long-term political strategy for disabled people', when these issues were clearly emerging in the 1990s and were precisely what we (yesterday's generation?) ought to have addressed, at the very least, in developing the movement's strategy? I think adding a wider perspective in the last paragraph, of the struggle disabled people need to face, with no suggestions is a 'cop out'.

CILs – what are they?

At least I made several attempts, from the 1990s onwards, for a route to get 'to be part of a far wider struggle to create a better society for all'. I argued that CILs should be developed so as to facilitate our own community-based services and profession. My view was that such an action flows from the social model of disability and has the potential of transforming ourselves and our place in society by making our own contribution to its development:

> First, the development of our own approaches to assistance not only requires an unpacking of the version imposed on us by people with abilities, but the creation of our own 'normal' forms of assistance. Our constructing of systematic forms of help according to our own social model of disability will generate new

services and service providers – professions allied to the community (PACs), as distinct from professions allied to medicine (PAMs). I believe that these workers will constitute our own trade union. It is these trade unionists, truly immersed in a disability culture, who will be a vital engine for social change. They will have a crucial role in promoting the national and international criticism of the dominant health and community care ideology that is not wanted by disabled people. (Finkelstein, 1999)

And in 2002:

Centres for Integrated Living (CILs) are one structure created by disabled people to service such aspirations and, in my view, workers in these centres are an embryonic profession allied to the community (PAC). This professionalisation process exactly replicates the progress made by women when they created their own midwifery service, rather than see themselves as woMEN with support needs wholly defined by males. User-generated support services create opportunities for harmonising user and provider needs and, at the very least, help to avoid the trap of disabled people being seen as disABLED, with support needs wholly defined by people with abilities. The allying of service development with community-based aspirations requires substantially different worker attitudes and guidelines for providing professional assistance. Setting up CIL services transforms the way disabled people think about themselves and the public identity they wish to cultivate. In my view this is the beginning of a journey in which a whole new cultural matrix of human relationships is waiting to be discovered. (Finkelstein, 2002)

And then again:

Our experiences in the emancipatory struggle, and in our development of CILs, have already thrown light on the kind of community based worker that we want, need and have to create. Inspired by insights from the radical social model of disability we must develop our own community based profession. This will provide an opening for disabled people and disenchanted professionals (especially OTs) to truly work together in creating a more appropriate nationalised service which allies itself with the community and responds to what people want. (Finkelstein, 2002)

The UK community support alternative?

Since the 1990s I made several attempts to highlight, not the dangers of promoting CILs, but the importance of understanding the difference between 'independent' and 'integrated' living. I wrote for example:

In addition to the pioneering 'Centres for *Integrated* Living' there were also 'Centres for *Independent* Living' in the UK more closely modelled on the USA

CIL brand. The fundamental difference between 'Centres for *Integrated* Living' and 'Centres for *Independent* Living' was sharply highlighted in the 1990s when the weight of national party politics shifted and the centre left Labour Party jumped over the central Liberal Democratic Party to occupy a centre right position, pushing the Conservative Party further to the right. This changed the political balance leaving no major national party with a 'socialist' agenda. Both the Derbyshire and Lambeth 'Centres for Integrated Living' were soon in crisis – the former became a 'Centre for *Inclusive* Living' and the latter was dismantled. On the other hand 'Centres for *Independent* Living', facing a greatly weakened ideological opposition within the 'disability movement' were now free to develop, rewrite history, and present their approach as the originator of CILs in the UK! (Finkelstein, 2004)

Apart from the substantial literature from Ken Davis, and others in Derbyshire, and Dick Leaman, and others in Lambeth, on the distinction between 'independent' and 'integrated' living services backed by myself, I know of no attempt to question the USA model for community-based services for disabled people. I find it extraordinary that people who campaigned so vigorously for the USA style of independent living services to be created in the expanding UK competitive market are now complaining that they are losing the government support upon which they are dependent! A leaflet announcing a demonstration on 2 September 2006 in support of new Independent Living Bill proclaimed:

Organisations of Disabled People are being made to close because of a lack of money and support . . . We will be dressed in rags and chains to show that it is still very hard to live independently because we do not have enough support to have freedom and choice.

So, after all, disabled people cannot be 'independent' without state 'support' – disabled people's 'independence' is 'dependent'!!! I don't think you have to be a psychologist to recognize the dominant message this demonstration will feed the 'non-disabled' public. The promoters of 'independent living' in a market economy can't complain that they get what they wanted (to the delight of privateers in the Blatcherite Labour Party). When disability groups became 'independent' they needed to get on with the job and *compete* against other 'independent living' service providers. If the competition happens to be well-established charities – well so be it – let the most competitive win! That's what 'independence' means in the capitalist system. It's all about 'efficient' service provision (meaning who has the cheapest product to sell). The market has no need for non-productive groups such as 'political' organizations of disabled people. In short, the disability movement is no longer setting the agenda for our emancipation – instead, we've become prisoners of a market that sets the agenda for our movement!

This is a capitalist dream come true – every single disabled person becomes an employer, pays personal assistants for their labour, is responsible for working conditions, ensures annual leave is provided, does the obligatory paperwork and checks taxes, etc. The only trouble is – capitalism doesn't stop here – competition means successful companies gobble up weaker groups, companies merge forming larger groups and those that fail, well, they go bankrupt and disappear. No surprise, surely, that entrepreneurs are setting up companies to relieve stressed disabled people from managing their 'direct payments' funding.

How can we carp about individuals or charities advertising their management services to disabled people getting 'direct payments'? If these new service providers are better able to advise disabled people and supply 'carers' than organizations of disabled people, such as CILs, they are only doing what people do in the market – competing! All I can say is that perhaps one day (when it dawns on people that a market in 'care' is not without stress for the recipients, the most efficient, or civilized) then the few successful monopolies in 'care' services will be nationalized and disabled people will be back where they started – with social services providing 'care' over which we have no control! Can we believe that people with capabilities would welcome being treated like an individual company when they use personal services? Imagine going to a restaurant and having to employ the waiter to 'care' for our needs (pay the person directly and do all the paperwork), then employ the cook to 'care' for food needs, etc. Well ... perhaps people once did have to do this until entrepreneurs started doing this for the customers and set up restaurants. Oh dear ...

Goodbye social model of disability?

The ideological problem facing the disability movement in the UK from the 1990s onwards was whether the social model of disability was still relevant in guiding our struggle or whether social changes had advanced so far that the original model no longer reflected the social context in which it had been created. Is the 'rights', or 'potpourri', model of disability now more in tune with the market economy expanding into the health and social services sector of society? Was the social model of disability really understood? Well ... as I wrote in 1996c: 'The adoption of Anti-Discrimination Legislation (ADL) is about to drive a wedge through the heart of the disabled community.'

And good riddance?

(written by Mike Oliver)

Unfortunately, as space does not permit, we can only make a brief response here. As was made clear in an earlier chapter of this book, we see the social model only as a tool. In our view it is not a social theory of disablement nor is it an explanation of what is happening to disabled people in capitalist society. We question the need to understand it in the way Vic outlines because, having earlier likened it to a hammer, we don't think it is necessary to understand the components of one in order to be able to knock a nail into a piece of wood. We do agree, however, that the legacy of the social model has been wasted; not because it wasn't properly understood but because it wasn't properly used.

We, like Vic, have always been critical of a rights-based approach to disability discrimination and have been vociferous in arguing that it should be part of a much broader strategy which includes the adequate resourcing of the disabled people's movement. We opposed those in the movement who argued that we should accept the Disability Discrimination Bill, which became the DDA in 1995, and argued that we should only accept fully comprehensive, properly enforceable rights legislation. We still believe that such acceptance was a mistake and, as we tried to make clear above, largely responsible for the difficulties that the movement now finds itself in.

The marketization of welfare, as Vic points out, has caused great difficulties for many disabled people but direct payments have also transformed the lives of some. We have supported them because professionalized welfare has regrettably proved to be incapable of giving disabled people control over the services we need to live a decent life. But we are also clear that we support Vic's vision of integrated rather than independent living as the basis for services with disabled people into the future. In fact, the first national care attendant scheme, which one of us was instrumental in developing (Oliver and Hasler, 1987), contains many of the elements of his description.

Vic is, of course, right to bring capitalism into focus in all these discussions and to point out that under such a regime disabled people will have to continue to beg for crumbs from the rich man's table or get others to beg on our behalf. While we share his vision of one day owning the table and equally sharing the food, what he doesn't address is that, in the meantime, we still have to eat.

10

Disablement into the Twenty-first Century

In 1999 I was invited by the University of Glasgow to give a lecture to celebrate the opening of their new Strathclyde Centre for Disability Research. I was delighted to accept and, as we were all going millennium crazy at the time, I decided to take as my theme the changing times for disabled people. I was, of course, aware that many years ago Bob Dylan had addressed this theme in one of his songs and so I decided to use the lecture both to explore my chosen theme and to pay homage to someone who was a key influence on my thinking.

It was my original intention to update this lecture, both in terms of the issues facing disabled people and new material that Bob Dylan has issued since then. However, after several aborted attempts I have decided to adopt a different approach as my tinkering destroys any sense of coherence in the piece and means I am unable to do justice to his work. So what I have decided to do instead is to leave it exactly as it is and provide an updating commentary at the end of the chapter discussing changing trends that have emerged in the decade since it was written. It is perhaps ironic that, a couple of years after my lecture, Dylan himself decided to return to the theme of the changing times with a song called 'Things Have Changed', which won him a Grammy for best song of the year.

~~~~~~~~~~

Disabled people and the inclusive society: or are the times really changing?

Come gather 'round people

As we approach the millennium the words inclusion and exclusion have become fashionable and are often used as shorthand to talk about a series of complex social processes. Like most words, they have the power to create meanings of their own and they are often used to suggest a new approach by society to a variety of disadvantaged and disaffected groups – a new dawn in the treatment of such groups for the new millennium. Whether these words really do represent a new approach or whether they are merely a cynical language game to misrepresent an unacceptable underlying reality that will continue into the millennium and beyond will be considered fully in this public lecture.

A recent publication jointly produced by Disabled Peoples International, Inclusion International, World Blind Union, World Federation of the Deaf and World Psychiatric Users Foundation to commemorate the 50th anniversary of the Universal Declaration of Human Rights is provocatively entitled 'Are Disabled People Included?'. In a foreword to the publication, Mary Robinson, United Nations Commissioner for Human Rights, states:

> disabled persons frequently live in deplorable conditions, owing to the presence of physical and social barriers which prevent their integration and full participation in the community. Millions of children and adults world-wide are segregated and deprived of their rights and are, in effect, living on the margins. This is unacceptable. (DAA, 1998, p. 2)

The United Nations itself estimates that the above quote applies to some 500 million disabled people across the world and, given that the UN declaration has been in existence for fifty years, it is clear that large numbers of disabled people have suffered human rights abuses for a long time. The report documents many of these abuses and names the perpetrators (or perps, as they are known in the American cop shows). The list of perps includes not just the usual suspects but also many of those governments who are so found of lecturing others about such abuses of human rights to the point of imposing trade sanctions, withdrawing economic aid or even bombing them into submission. Unable to resist the temptation to play language games myself, this report reveals that many of those who wish to appear as whiter than white could do with a good wash themselves.

I was delighted to be invited to give this lecture because it has given me the opportunity to think again about my own attempts to understand what has happened to disabled people, what is currently happening to us and what may happen in the future. Accordingly, I wish to pay homage to the writer who has been the most influential in my own thinking and writing about the exclusion and inclusion of disabled people; not Karl Marx, as those of you familiar with my work might assume, but Bob Dylan. Some forty years ago, and for another troubled time, he wrote a song *The Times They Are A-changing'*. Like many great writers, his work is timeless and the message in that particular song is perhaps more pertinent now, as we approach the millennium, than it was when he wrote it. In it he warned us all:

> If your time to you
> Is worth savin'
> Then you better start swimmin'
> Or you'll sink like a stone
> For the times they are a-changing'
>
> (From *The Times They Are A-Changin'*
> Lyrics by Bob Dylan
> Copyright © 1963; renewed 1991 Special Rider Music
> Administered by Sony/ATV Music Publishing
> All rights reserved. Used by permission.)

Drawing lines and counting curses

My own deliberations on the exclusion of disabled people from modern societies unequivocally locates capitalism as the main villain. While I don't think Bob Dylan ever used the term, in my favourite song of his, *It's Alright Ma, I'm Only Bleeding'*, he is clearly talking about capitalist society when he says:

> the masters make the rules
> For the wise men and the fools.
>
> (From *It's Alright, Ma (I'm Only Bleeding)*
> Lyrics by Bob Dylan
> Copyright © 1965; renewed 1993 Special Rider Music
> Administered by Sony/ATV Music Publishing
> All rights reserved. Used by permission.)

And he sums up the central values of capitalism in one line, 'money doesn't talk, it swears'.

Unpopular and unfashionable it may be in these (post)modern times to use such terms, it does still seem to me that capitalism has a lot to answer for. For example, for fifty years the people of the Balkans lived fairly happy and peaceful lives until they were 'liberated' by the coming of free market capitalism. I do not make this point as a quick and easy comment on what is currently happening there, nor as a cheap jibe at capitalism. But it is relevant to the theme of disability in that war is responsible for creating thousands of impaired people every year all over the world and using euphemisms like 'collateral damage' shouldn't be allowed to obscure that fact.

But, to return to the theme of the exclusion of disabled people, while a comprehensive history and anthropology of disability has yet to be written it is clear from what evidence we do have that disabled people are not excluded from all societies. Accordingly, exclusion is not an intrinsic part of the human condition of being disabled. Even in those many societies that do exclude disabled people, this exclusion varies with the economic and social conditions and the core values of the society concerned. Forms of exclusion range from death-making through expulsion, onto institutionalization and, finally, to denial.

In our own society, disabled people have and continue to face all these forms of exclusion. We know the Nazis killed 200,000 disabled people in Germany, but we still practice death-making in the here and now and still hidden from view. Disabled children and elderly people are the main victims, and we avert our eyes just like the Germans did all those years ago.

We still practice expulsion by denying disabled people the right to live where and how they choose and we claim that we cannot afford to do otherwise. We still build and place people in institutions and attempt to salvage our consciences by calling them group homes, residential care or old people's homes. We continue to deny that these practices are happening and we even name these institutions after the perps of this exclusion; there are Cheshire homes all over the world, for example, and in our own localities we glorify such places by calling them after the local politicians and bigwigs responsible for building them.

And we play yet more language games with our discussions of rationing and economic priorities and we invent code words like QUALYS and DALYS to disguise our unacceptable activities and the choices that are already being made, hidden from our eyes. Usually, it falls to great artists like Bob Dylan to point to the realities underpinning these games. But this is not always the case; the power of words sometimes emerges out of profound experience like the one Ann Macfarlane describes in her poem 'Watershed'. Let's not play language games any more:

> We were quiet, hiding our fear
> Knowing in our nine-year-old hearts

That we were about to witness something
Frightening and evil.
One cried quietly,
And we clutched inadequate towels around our thin bodies
As Mary, pretty and small, passive and unmoving
Became the focus of all our attention.

They lifted her effortlessly
Into the deep porcelain tub
And then, without warning
Pushed her passive pale body under the water
And held her there.
We felt the fear through our ill clad bodies.

There was no shriek, no cry, no dramatic action.
The loud clock ticked on
A reminder that we had seen this before,
Had shivered and cried restlessly
And watched Mary come up again.
Now we were two weeks more knowing
And understood that we must not move,
Must not show what we felt.

Mary was dead.
Her body naked in the porcelain bathtub,
Tiny, frail, utterlessly lifeless.
Her long wavy hair over her face not pretty any more.
She needed to be hugged, needed to be cared for.
But her bathers had no compassion.
They stood motionless over her, Eyes staring transfixed
Not seeing a human child, not seeing her.

Slowly their attention turned to us,
Unacknowledged, unwanted onlookers.
One by one we were wheeled back to our beds
Alone with our fearful thoughts.
No one spoke of Mary again.
It was if she had never been,
And yet she was our friend,
Part of our lives.

Nearly fifty years later, this scene comes and visits me.
Then we knew we must stay silent.
Now I speak it for all the Marys

In institutions, in hospitals, in segregated schools
And for my nine-year-old self, who had no choice
But to sit and watch.
                    (Macfarlane, in Keith, 1994)

In face of the anger that such words stir, 'why did such things happen?' hardly seems an appropriate question, but we owe it to all the future Mary's to ask the question because the killing of disabled children is not just a thing of the past but something that continues into the present.

Our continued, and continuing, exclusion from the world of work is the most important factor in what happens to us and the way we are treated by society. The coming of industrialism shook many groups and individuals out of the labour force and they became burdens on society in general and the taxpayer in particular. As a consequence, society had to do something about disabled people and it did, not being shy about using all the forms of exclusion mentioned above. However, it needed people to sanction and carry out these exclusionary practices and it found the increasingly powerful medical profession and the newly emerging ideology of individualism willing supporters. I'm not, of course, arguing that disabled people are or have been treated better in other kinds of society, but I'm here to talk about us today and not others or yesterday.

This is obviously a very simplified version of a complex argument about exclusion that I published some ten years ago (Oliver, 1990). It has not been without its critics and revisionists of one kind or another. You pay too much attention to work and not enough to culture, say some. Society's hatred of us is because we are classed as 'other', not because we are unable to work, say others. You fail to allow for the personal limitations that impairments bring with them, say yet others. Pernicious social forces such as sexism, racism, homophobia and ageism are more important than work in our lives, say yet more critics. And even if what you say is true, the coming of the welfare state and the development of community care will eventually ensure the inclusion of disabled people because they will be taken care of, so the final argument goes.

I do not deny the relevance or force of some of these arguments in shaping the lives of disabled people, but ultimately I still believe, like Karl Marx, we are what we do, not what we think. On encountering a stranger for the first time and struggling for something to say, we usually open with the question 'And what do you do?' To ask that same stranger 'What are you thinking?' would be liable to evoke a very strange response indeed. If you doubt my word, the next time you meet a stranger do what the American sociologist Harold Garfinkel used to encourage his students to do and disrupt the unspoken rules and norms of everyday life. Conduct your very own sociological fieldwork and start asking complete strangers what they are thinking. However, please don't write to me with the results or try to sue me if you get punched on the nose.

To be constantly and consistently denied the opportunity to work, to make a material contribution to the well being of society, is to be positioned as not being fully human, indeed, in my view, is the root cause of us being labelled as 'other' or *Useless Eaters*, as the title of Simon Smith's CD suggests. And our culture only allows us to be Christopher Reeve or Christy Brown precisely because we are not fully involved in working in all those industries that produce images about us. Racism and sexism further separate us from our humanness when they attempt to deny a disabled woman the right to mother the child she has given birth to or a young black man the wish to have his hair groomed the way he chooses. Finally, the welfare state tells us not to worry because, even if we are a burden on carers, we will still be cared for – by that vast professional army or our loved ones who work tirelessly on our behalf, rather than allowing us the dignity to work for ourselves and, indeed, to become ourselves. Will it all be different after the millennium? Are the times really changing for disabled people?

Prophesies of the pen

To return to the main theme of this lecture, that of inclusion, it is certainly something that the new Labour government has discovered. Led by the nose to it by one of their (alleged) gurus, Professor Tony Giddens, who in his new book called *The Third Way* suggests that 'The new politics defines equality as inclusion and inequality as exclusion' (Giddens, 1998, p. 102). And he further suggests that, 'Equality must contribute to diversity, not stand in its way' (Giddens, 1998, p. 100). Personally, I prefer my own guru's thoughts on the little matter of equality:

> A self-ordained professor's tongue
> Too serious to fool
> Spouted out that liberty
> Is just equality in school
> 'Equality', I spoke the word
> As if a wedding vow.

Ah, but I was so much older then,
I'm younger than that now.

(From *My Back Pages*
Lyrics by Bob Dylan
Copyright © 1964; renewed 1992 Special Rider Music
Administered by Sony/ATV Music Publishing
All rights reserved. Used by permission.)

The government, of course, despite Tony Blair's claim to be an old rock 'n' roller, prefers to listen to their own guru rather than mine and has recently published their own thoughts on exclusion and inclusion:

> The causes of social exclusion are varied and complex and often cut across traditional Government boundaries. Many of the individuals and communities affected by social exclusion are on the receiving end of many separate public programmes and professional services. The poor rarely have the chance of helping to determine the programme of action for themselves. These programmes are rarely integrated; most deal with symptoms rather than causes; and most have been driven by the structure of existing Government machinery rather than by the needs of citizens. Not surprisingly, these approaches have often been ineffective. (HMSO, 1998, p. 63)

Can we take them at their word 'as if it were a wedding vow'? Their claim, for example, to provide a 'joined-up' approach to tackling the problems of exclusion cannot be squared with their failure to repeal the Disability Discrimination Act. How can outlawing discrimination in some areas of the labour market and not in education or transport be joined up? How can disabled people compete properly in the labour market if they continue to be denied an education that gives them the necessary qualifications so to do or they are unable to get to work once they have found a job?

Mrs Hodge, the new Minister for Disabled People, offers no more hope. In her new regular column for that disability rag that passes for the disabled version of the *Sun* she makes no promises to provide fully comprehensive and fully enforceable civil rights legislation but instead promises to change permanently the climate of opinion towards disabled people by fully involving a combination of newspaper moguls, business, the Royal Institutes, one-legged models and fading television personalities, many of whom most of us thought were dead. Haven't we heard all this for the last fifty years and hasn't it proved to be an abject failure?

As far as I know, Bob Dylan has never met Margaret Hodge, but he once wrote a song about another woman who got up his nose in the way she gets up mine:

> I see you got your brand new leopard-skin pill box hat
> Well, you must tell me, baby
> How your head feels under something like that
> Under your brand new leopard-skin pill box hat
> Well you look so pretty in it
> Honey, can I jump on it sometime?
>
> (From *Leopard-Skin Pill Box Hat*
> Lyrics by Bob Dylan
> Copyright © 1966; renewed 1994 Dwarf Music
> Administered by Sony/ATV Music Publishing
> All rights reserved. Used by permission.)

There is one area where the government's very own guru does agree with me, and that is that work serves many important purposes, both for the individual and society, and that we must create a proper balance between work and non-work:

> Involvement in the labour force, and not just in dead end jobs, is plainly vital to attacking involuntary exclusion. Work has multiple benefits: it generates income for the individual, gives a sense of stability and direction in life, and creates wealth for the overall society. Yet inclusion must stretch well beyond work, not only because there are many people at any one time not able to be in the labour force, but because a society too dominated by the work ethic would be a thoroughly unattractive place in which to live. An inclusive society must provide for the basic needs of those who can't work, and must recognise the wider diversity of goals that life has to offer. (Giddens, 1998, p. 110)

The government agrees, and in the white paper 'A New Contract For Welfare' they promise a new 'welfare to work' deal for disabled people and suggest that up to a million disabled people can be moved off welfare and into work, thus substantially shifting the burden away from social security and thereby enabling these disabled people to pay taxes instead; to refer back to my earlier comments, to reposition themselves as citizens rather than to continue to be seen as burdens on the state. A noble aim, which has been somewhat tarnished in its implementation: while the Government intends to lop £750 million off benefits for disabled people immediately, so far only fifty disabled people have found jobs under the new deal. Personally, I'd settle for

750,000 disabled people into work and £50 million off social security benefits. Expecting a combination of vested interests, charities, cripples and the near-dead to solve this really does seem to be little more than 'blowing in the wind'.

The problem is that the government's plans to get disabled people into work are focused around two initiatives: a small number of special schemes and job coaches for individual disabled people. At a conservative estimate, there are a least a million disabled people of working age who are employable and such trifles are unlikely to have any significant impact on the unemployment rate among disabled people. They also claim that they will address the issue of equality of opportunity in the workplace, but they have no plans to introduce fully comprehensive civil rights legislation and the new Disability Rights Commission will only have an enforcement role in the small number of cases where issues of principle are at stake. If equality (of opportunity) is indeed a wedding vow for the government, it is truly fortunate that disabled people are 'so much younger now' and we know that the politicians are playing language games of their own.

Giddens, in the above quote, recognizes that work may no longer be available for everyone who requires or wants it and that a genuinely inclusive society must provide for the needs of those who don't work, for whatever reason. Other gurus, notably Zygmunt Bauman – one of the gurus of postmodernism, have gone further and suggested that, into the millennium and beyond, society will be driven by the consumption ethic rather than the work ethic (Bauman, 1998). While I remain to be convinced about this, when discussing this proposition with my friend Merav recently, she assures me that she is no longer what she does but what she shops and that she only does what she does so that she can shop.

To put this sociologically, if consumption rather than production is to become a basis for identity formation, then governments may need to adopt some radically different social policies. Bauman suggests that the decoupling of income from employment is one such policy. Disabled people in Britain will recognize an earlier version of this policy when, in the late 1960s and early 1970s, the Disablement Income Group and the Disability Alliance proposed a national disability income available as of right to all disabled people. This proposal was not simply attacked on the grounds of cost but disabled people themselves argued that such a proposal would serve as a basis for the further exclusion of disabled people from other parts of society (UPIAS, 1976); if disabled people didn't need jobs, why bother to educate them or give them the means to travel – so the argument went. If governments were to adopt decoupling policies, not just for disabled people, but for everyone else as well, then clearly the basis of the arguments around a national disability income would shift considerably. But until then, while participation in the world of work remains the main mechanism for social inclusion, disabled people will continue quite rightly to demand a full and equal share of it.

The link between work and exclusion is clearly important as far as older people are concerned, many of whom are disabled for, as Tony Giddens notes (1998, p. 120), 'A society that separates older people from the majority in a retirement ghetto cannot be called inclusive.' More than one in six older people will spend the last years of their lives in these 'retirement ghettos' and, as I grow older every year, I get more and more scared that such a fate waits for me. As usual, Bob Dylan expresses this so much better than I can:

> The ghetto that you build for me is the one you end up in.

(From *Dead Man Dead Man*
Lyrics by Bob Dylan
Copyright © 1981 Special Rider Music
Administered by Sony/ATV Music Publishing
All rights reserved. Used by permission.)

Small wonder that the Direct Action Network (DAN) can claim that 'residential nursing home beds are on the increase, abuse in institutions is rife and our people are paying through the nose for it, selling their homes for nursing profits'. They warn that they 'are going to build a freedom railroad out of the institutions and into the community'.

Heading for the highlands

Will any of us actually 'be released' with the coming of the millennium? Bob Dylan aficionados will note that so far I have drawn on his early work but his most recent CD includes a eulogy to Scotland. However, like most of his work, the words are about much more than Scotland; they are about that special place that we all have in our hearts or heads to which we give a variety of names – heaven, utopia, home, socialism and so on. In our own way we are all heading for our own highlands.

The decline in religion and the demise of state socialism have dented somewhat our faith in the existence of both heavenly and earthly utopias and if we do have a vision for the future, it is to science, technology and medicine that we look for our salvation. Science will provide us with the knowledge to change the world, technology the means to accomplish it and medicine will ensure that we are healthy enough and remain alive long enough to enjoy it, so the argument goes.

At the interface of these worlds of science, technology and medicine is the issue of genetics. Its promoters say it will eradicate all illnesses and impairments and will prolong life for us all, or rather for all of us who are genetically perfect. The rest will be genetically engineered out of existence, for their own good as well as that of society. It sounds a familiar story, doesn't it? Disabled people will be confined to the history books and occasionally in the new millennium films like *Elephant Man* will be made about our wretched lives and their makers will probably win the twenty-first-century equivalent of Oscars. Everyone will live healthy, pain-free lives and life-expectancy figures will continue to increase.

Not everyone sees this as heading for the highlands, of course. Some see it as heading for the lowlands (not, in this instance, the place where the sad-eyed lady Bob Dylan once wrote about came from), both because of the global ecological crisis that has been created by science and technology and the concern over what genetically perfect individuals will really mean for society. Many disabled people fear that their disappearance from the future will not be a matter of progress but one of bitter regret, for society as well as for ourselves. When, nearly twenty years ago in the pages of the *Guardian*, I claimed that my disability was the best thing that ever happened to me, I was metaphorically burned at the stake by being grilled by Dr Miriam Stoppard on live television. Fortunately, since then a positive politics of personal identity has emerged and more and more disabled people don't want to change the way we are any more.

This identity politics does not merely provide a personal plea to allow us to stay alive but suggests that difference makes a positive contribution to the ultimate health and well being of society. Let me give you a historical example. One of the conditions it is claimed will be eradicated by the appliance of genetic science is that of Huntington's chorea. If that technology had been available, say a hundred years ago, one Woodrow Wilson Guthrie would not have been born. In that case, he would not have inspired Bob Dylan to produce the work he did and, as a consequence of that, I would not be here before you now, giving this public lecture.

Some of you will undoubtedly say, 'Good thing too; that's the best argument for genetic engineering that I can think of,' but that would be to miss the serious point that when we tamper with such things it effects us all. Even the heir to the British monarchy has recently fuelled the current moral panic about genetically modified food by pointing to its potential dangers. I await the day when he will express similar concerns about genetically modified people. It would perhaps be too cynical a commentary on modern politics to suggest such a question will never be asked because the power of the medical establishment is so much greater than the farmers' lobby these days. Nevertheless, ask yourselves what scares you most – eating a genetically modified carrot or sleeping with a cloned person?

The slow and the fast

However, it is not just cynicism that is bringing about a decline in people's faith about modern politics and its institutions. It is also fuelled by greedy, selfish and hypocritical politicians themselves, as well as the failure of the state to deliver programmes based upon the democratic wishes of the people. How else can we account for the fact that it took the British political system more than fifteen years to deliver anti-discrimination legislation (albeit in a watered-down form) when everyone from the general public and leader writers in the *Sun*, to elected politicians and disabled people, was in favour of it. What's more, this failure will not be resolved, in my view, by finding 'a third way' between state socialism and market freedom; the decline in modern politics is much more serious than that.

Once again, Bob Dylan puts it much better than I could:

> The line it is drawn
> The curse it is cast
> The slow one now
> Will later be fast
> As the present now
> Will later be past
> The order is rapidly fadin'.
> And the first one now
> Will later be last
> For the times they are a-changin'.

They certainly are for disabled people. In the last thirty years we have begun to shake off the dead hand of charity that has kept us oppressed and excluded for more than 150 years and to confront all those politicians who have offered us little but patronizing benevolence while continuing to build their own careers. In so doing, we have built a political and social movement that does offer us the very real possibility of 'changing our futures' (Campbell and Oliver, 1996). This possibility is based upon the bedrock of three big ideas, which have emerged exclusively from our movement and have been based entirely on our own experiences; the ideas are, of course, the social model of disability, independent living and civil rights.

We are already seeing some of the benefits of this in terms of service delivery with the establishment of independent living schemes and centres, the coming of direct payments and the acceptance in principle, if not in practice, of the idea of civil rights. As a consequence, more and more disabled people are escaping from institutions, others are regaining some semblance of control over such mundane things as when to go to bed and get up, what to eat and when, and yet others are taking back control over their lives completely. We should not, however, be fooled into thinking that these are the majority of disabled people either here in Britain or elsewhere throughout the world.

While we may be 'heading for the highlands', there is still a long way to go and many barriers to face. Most recently, for example, we have seen some changes to the leadership in some of the organizations who make up the disabled people's movement in Britain and this has been seized upon by our enemies to suggest that somehow the whole movement is in crisis. We have to remember that those organizations that seek to dance on the grave of our movement are those very organizations who, in the past, kept us excluded and oppressed and who now seek to pass off our big ideas as if they were their own.

The chimes of freedom

It would not be appropriate for me to end this public lecture, organized by the Strathclyde Centre for Disability Research, without some reference to the role of academia in ensuring the inclusion of disabled people in the third millennium. From small beginnings more than twenty years ago, disability studies has secured a small place on the agenda and in the curricula of some universities and we can be confident that from these small beginnings will emerge a vibrant force for educational and social change. We can be confident about this because

disability studies is developing as a genuine partnership between disabled people and academia and, as a consequence of this, the voice of
disabled people will be heard far louder than it otherwise might.

While the relationship between academia and disabled people will
not always be an easy one, nonetheless it will be fruitful. If nothing
else, it will allow the voice of disabled people to be heard in fora where
otherwise it would not, and I am confident that the Strathclyde Centre
for Disability Research will play a role in giving the disabled people of
Strathclyde a voice. It is not, however, only academics who give voice
to the voiceless in pursuit of freedom, but great artistes as well. I will
end where I began, with the words of Bob Dylan who in this verse
manages to acknowledge the difficulties and the potential of giving
voice to the voiceless as well as mentioning disabled people:

> Through the wild cathedral evening the rain unraveled tales
> For the disrobed faceless forms of no position
> Tolling for the tongues with no place to bring their thoughts
> All down in taken-for-granted situations
> Tolling for the deaf an' blind, tolling for the mute
> Tolling for the mistreated, mateless mother, the mistitled prostitute
> For the misdemeanour outlaw, chased an' cheated by pursuit
> An' we gazed upon the chimes of freedom flashing.

Let's make sure the chimes of freedom really do ring out for disabled
people in the third millennium.

Things have changed (in) modern times

As I said in the Introduction to this chapter, I decided not to make
any changes to the original chapter but to add this commentary at
the end. While I am happy with the way the chapter reads, it needs
me to add this commentary because there have been some significant
changes since it was originally written. There are also things that have
remained the same since the original lecture. I will briefly discuss five
issues herein, issues that I have already discussed elsewhere in the book
or that I will return to in the final chapter.

The first issue focuses on government and politics. In the lecture I drew attention to a major report produced by five of the largest and most respected international disability organizations where they accuse many nations of allowing disabled people to live in deplorable conditions and lead intolerable lives. What is different about this report is that it names names, and many leading nations are indicted therein. At the time of writing this commentary, we are subjected to the sight of these countries hectoring the Chinese government over its human rights record and threatening action over the Beijing Olympics while continuing to do as much trade with them as possible. It's enough to give government and politics a bad name.

And its not just collective politics that deserves a bad name. In the lecture I use a Dylan song to criticize the then Minister for Disabled People. I have to confess that all the subsequent incumbents have got up my nose too. I have lost count of the number of conferences and meetings on disability I have attended over the years where the Minister turns up (often late), ignores the other speakers, makes a short, patronizing speech, which only demonstrates their ignorance, announces a small grant or irrelevant government initiative and then leaves before they can be asked any questions. If individual politicians continue to reduce disability politics to a series of public relations exercises then they shouldn't be surprised if people jump on their 'leopard-skin pill box hats'.

The second issue concerns the Disability Discrimination Act. When the Labour government came to power it made it clear that it would not abolish the Act and replace it with something better, despite promises to do so when in opposition. Initially, it was also reluctant to amend the legislation, but over the years some changes have been forced upon them. These enforced amendments have not made it an effective piece of legislation, however, and it has failed most notably in getting disabled people into the workforce in any significant numbers. Testament to this is the failure of the current administration to implement properly any meaningful welfare-to-work programme for disabled people, although it continues to talk about it and even promise it. In the original lecture, I pointed to the flaws in their 1998 plans and the current plans contain exactly the same flaws.

The third issue concerns the way we treat older people in society. Elsewhere in this book I have already discussed my own fears about ageing, and the unpalatable fact is that, since the original lecture, little has changed for older people. Despite government claims of increased funding to improve social care for elderly people, many still end up unwillingly in residential care or barely surviving with inadequate community services. The establishment of variously named 'standards commissions' has done little to improve this situation for older people at least, though the job prospects of many middle-class professionals have been advanced. Those who think the big charities have really changed would do well to note the lack of righteous anger and indignation coming from organizations for older people at this appalling situation and would do well to remember that ' the ghetto you build for me will be the one you end up in'. After all, we will all start 'shrinking' one day.

I must admit that in the original lecture I was over-optimistic about the future of the disabled people's movement and its ability to promote independent living. I also underestimated the ability of the big charities to reinvent themselves. If they had approached the task of improving the lives of disabled people with the same energy and imagination they have used to ensure their own survival, perhaps I would be eating my own words about them now. This has already been discussed in more detail in the previous chapter and will be returned to in the next.

The fourth issue concerns the progress of science. Earlier in this edition I pointed to the fact that the claims of medical science to eradicate impairments have become more muted because claims of 'cures just round the corner' can only be made until the corner is actually turned. At the time of the lecture, the Human Genome Project was the current claimant but we appear to have turned that corner without any cures arriving. The latest claimant appears to be stem cell research, which is not without its share of political controversy. In the current arguments, disabled people are used by both sides to justify their positions, although, as usual, without consulting us about it.

The final issue I wish to draw attention to is my comments about the future of disability studies. Based upon my assumption of a continuing and strengthening relationship with the disabled people's movement to the benefit of both, I was wildly optimistic about future progress. My predictions have not turned out to be accurate in this respect, but I shall reserve my explanation (defence) to the next and final chapter.

11

Personalizing the Political and Politicizing the Personal

Introduction

The final chapter of the first edition examined the issue of the relationship between the individual and the collective. This relationship is an issue for all political and social movements, for social theory, social policy and service development; all topics which have been discussed extensively in this book. It also raises the question of the relationship between the processes of individual and collective empowerment which leads to the crux of political life itself, the relationship between individual and social action. I want to return to these issues here, but in the light of changing circumstances of the last decade, in particular the decline in the power and influence of the disabled people's movement which has been accompanied by the resurrection of the big charities who have built a formidable alliance with newly created government organizations, such as the Disability Rights Commission (which has now become the Equalities and Human Rights Commission) and the Office for Disability Issues.

Those involved now use the term 'disability movement' to talk about this alliance, but my preferred term for it is 'disabling corporatism'. This might seem an unnecessarily pejorative term for individuals and organizations who are working on behalf of disabled people but there are two reasons for me choosing it. First, as I pointed out earlier in my discussion of research, acting on behalf of disabled people rather than acting under our control inevitably positions us as incapable of acting on our own behalf. Second, as I pointed out in my discussion of education, when I used a quote from Roger Slee, good intentions do not always ensure the right outcomes.

In the earlier edition of this book I used Gramsci's distinction between positional and organic intellectuals because I wanted to find a way of examining the individual/collective relationship in the process of attempting to build a movement for collective empowerment. I had hoped that this would enable all involved to talk about important issues of individual and collective leadership without resorting to personal attacks and the settling of old scores, real and imagined. Unfortunately, this has proved not to be the case, so for this new edition I shall attempt to use the concept of 'instrumentalism' to discuss the tension between the individual and the collective in disabling corporatism, in the disabled people's movement and in disability studies. I do not use this particular concept in a pejorative sense but as a way of highlighting the personal, professional and political choices open to people struggling to produce a better life for disabled people.

Personalizing the political in disabling corporatism

There is no doubt that over the last decade the big charities have experienced a resurgence, while the power and influence of the disabled people's movement has undoubtedly declined. As I have pointed out in this book, these two things are not unconnected, both because the greater resources of the big charities have enabled them to compete more effectively for government and local contracts and because they have unashamedly stolen the ideas of the disabled people's movement and learned to use its language. This has been helped by the increasing numbers of disabled people who have moved into key positions in many of these organizations. Ironically, many of those disabled people would not have 'touched any of these organizations with the proverbial barge pole' ten years ago.

In the first edition of this book, I drew attention to Jenny Morris's explanation for this phenomenon:

> Those disabled people who ally themselves with organisations for disabled people do so predominantly because their class position leads them to fear radical change. Some of us may feel a sense of outrage at how such disabled people are used to give legitimacy to the organisations which do so much to oppress disabled people. We must also recognise, however, that internalised oppression exerts a tremendous influence. A disabled person who holds a position within a conservative charitable organisation has been told all their lives – as we all have – how inadequate and pitiable disabled people are. Small wonder then that such people, when asked to involve more disabled people in their organisation, commonly respond that there isn't any capable person with the relevant expertise amongst the disabled community. (Morris, 1991, p. 177)

However, I would suggest that this explanation is no longer adequate to account for the numbers or kinds of people now allied to these organizations, some of whom had come from prominent positions within the disabled people's movement and others who had studied disability at one of the increasing number of universities offering disability studies courses of one kind or another.

The 'internalized oppression' explanation no longer fits the fact that many of those individuals are well aware of what these organizations represent and have only allied themselves to them after a great deal of soul searching. The first group of these individuals is made up of what I would call 'political instrumentalists', in that they recognize the political realities of the current situation and think that the best way to improve the lives of disabled people, in the short term at least, is to ally themselves to these organizations. The second group is what I would call 'economic instrumentalists', who decide, often after they have fought their way through an education system that has continually discriminated against them, that they can only further their careers by joining those organizations who have the resources available to employ them.

I'm not suggesting here that these individuals are motivated only by political power or money; I recognize that they often only join these organizations after coming to a considered decision. While I personally may disagree with that decision and think it is misguided, they would argue that it is only a recognition of political and economic realities; after all, things have got to be changed, rents and mortgages need to be paid and families fed. I certainly respect these decisions and think that some of the personal attacks that they have been subjected to are unwarranted. Only history will show who is right and who is wrong and, for my part as I have admitted in this book, my ability to predict future trends is not very good.

In his contribution to this book Vic Finkelstein takes me to task for 'studiously avoiding' naming those individuals who he regards as acting against the interests of disabled people, and accuses me of 'copping out'. It is true that I have always tried to avoid criticizing individuals personally but I have savagely attacked their ideas and views if I disagree with them. A few years ago I went as far as calling for an end to arguments within the disabled people's movement because the arguments had degenerated into little more than personal abuse (Oliver, 2003). In fact I must admit that I find myself, somewhat uncomfortably, agreeing with Shakespeare:

> Our real enemy is not individuals, but the system which divides us, which creates our disability, which makes it possible for others to profit from our

exclusion: it's convenient and easy to highlight people, but the focus of our rage and our action should be the structures. (Shakespeare, 1993, p. 32)

Having said that I do not believe in singling people out, I now propose to do so, not to attack personally but to illuminate some of the difficulties when the political becomes too personal. I have known Bert Massie for more than thirty years, during which time he was Assistant Director, and later Director, of the Royal Association of Disability and Rehabilitation (RADAR) and subsequently Chair of the Disability Rights Commission (DRC). During that time I have shared numerous platforms with him where we have discussed and disputed our differing ideas. When I started teaching my postgraduate course in disability studies in Canterbury, Bert was always on the list of external speakers making contributions to the course. He was always clear in his discussions with my students that he thought working from the inside was more politically productive than criticizing from the outside. To paraphrase former American president Lyndon B. Johnson, 'he preferred to be inside the tent pissing out rather than outside the tent pissing in'.

He has continued to operate from within the tent and there have been some gains from this. Earlier, I called Vic Finkelstein 'the pied piper of the disabled people's movement' and I regard Bert Massie as 'the midwife of the social model of disability'. When he was Assistant Director at RADAR in the early 1980s he organized a conference in Bath and invited me to be one of the speakers. It was at this conference that I publicly launched the social model of disability upon an unsuspecting audience. Later in the same decade, by now as Director of RADAR, he provided the 'seed money' to Stephen Bradshaw, then Director of the Spinal Injuries Association (SIA), and myself to put together the research proposal on anti-discrimination legislation to the Joseph Rowntree Foundation. This later became the publication (Barnes, 1991) that was responsible for the then government changing its mind about the need for anti-discrimination legislation.

I'm not claiming that he was responsible for either of those things but, that by working from the inside, he was able to help along two developments that are an important part of the history of the disabled people's movement. Others may want (and have) to make jokes about him on the disability cabaret circuit and call him the government's poodle in print, but all that is at stake here is a disagreement over political tactics. I regret the fact that collectively, as disabled people, we have been unable to create a movement that sustains and nurtures people of different political persuasions without allowing genuine arguments and debates to spill over into vituperative personal attacks.

In my discussion of this in the earlier edition I was hopeful that the commonality of experiences of oppression in the disabling society would have allowed us to build an inclusive movement, but, sadly, this appears not to be the case. I realize that this makes me sound more like a woolly liberal than the Stalinist many people think I am, but I believe that personalizing the political views and tactics of others is not just wrong but also counter-productive. What's more, given a different set of circumstances, I cannot be sure that I would not have become a political or economic instrumentalist. When I finished my PhD I spent a year unemployed and was either ignored or turned down for more than 150 jobs. With my self-esteem at an all-time low, a young family to feed and a mortgage to pay, if one of the big charities had offered me a job who's to say I wouldn't have accepted it. To paraphrase Karl Marx, 'Our existence determines our consciousness, not the other way round.'

Personalizing the political in the disabled people's movement

When organizations emerge out of the reinterpretation of personal experience as political, as is the case with the feminist movement, black struggles and the disabled people's movement, then the tension between individuals and the collectivity becomes a crucial issue. It is a tension between the organization becoming bureaucratic and oligarchical and remaining democratic and rooted in the personal experiences of its membership. To put it bluntly, as social movements become more successful, so the leadership become more prominent and:

> 'Prominent personalities' are seen to have a destructive effect on the attempt by the movements to create credible alternatives to prevailing political structures. The usefulness of intellectual inspirers is questioned by activists who draw the distinction between the capacity of such people to generate publicity for the movement and the practical skills required by militants engaged in a locally based social struggle. (Papadakis, 1993, p. 90)

Earlier, I alluded to the suspicion that the disabled people's movement has had towards individuals in leadership positions. Many years ago, the issue of prominent personalities was one of the major bones of contention between UPIAS and the Disability Alliance. The Alliance wanted a small group of expert 'intellectuals' to speak on behalf of disabled people, which was, in itself, seen as a threat. Reflecting on this after some years, Finkelstein argued:

> I regarded it as important to draw attention to this as a potential threat to the movement. This was because any strategy which gave credibility to a single issue approach, such as the incomes approach, could divert the energy and attention of disabled people away from the task of organisation building into the dead end of supporting the experts as they write about and present their arguments for the rank and file. (Finkelstein, 1994)

Within the disabled people's movement, there has also been some discussion of the role of people without impairments (or people with abilities, as Vic Finkelstein has, somewhat ironically, called them). This has usually centred on the role of 'allies' within the movement and, crucial to this, the ability to identify who is, and who is not, an ally. Holdsworth, while admitting there is a role for allies within the movement, takes a fairly trenchant view of who they might be:

> Disabled people, for our sins, encounter a whole range of people throughout our lives; parents, carers, brothers, sisters, professionals like doctors, nurses, OTs, social workers – even celebrities who sometimes 'adopt us'. Are they our allies? Many will think so and some will be surprised to find out that, not only are they not our allies, but, in fact, are the beast itself. (Holdsworth, 1993, p. 4)

The role of allies has not been much discussed in more recent times, despite my attempts in the first edition of this book to find a less emotive way of talking about it. In reality, with the coming of disabling corporatism, there has been an unspoken assumption that we, disabled people and those with abilities, are all on the same side. However, recently the issue has surfaced again as part of a public relations attempt to justify the fact that disabling corporatism has awarded itself £4.2 million to 'capacity-build disabled people's organizations'. According to Andy Rickell, a past executive director at SCOPE and a prime mover in the capacity-building project, the word 'ally' signifies a new, positive role for those involved whom he calls 'corporate allies'. The public relations stunt obviously has worked because several organizations controlled by disabled people have joined the project. Whether these organizations have become part of disabling corporatism or whether they have taken the money to pursue their own agendas remains to be seen.

At the same time, another spokesperson for disabling corporatism, as well as achieving promotion from the now defunct Disability

Rights Commission onto the Equality and Human Rights Commission, decided to promote himself to the role of adviser to the disability movement, as he calls it. He (Crowther, 2007) advises the disabled people's movement to drop its ideological purity, to recognize that times have changed and to cooperate with its corporate allies. The problem is that the disabled people's movement has never been ideologically pure; the changes he alludes to have had little effect on the lives of disabled people; and that disabling corporatism has stolen our ideas and denied us the resources to pursue the agendas he now claims as his own (Oliver and Barnes, 2008). If this is the best advice our 'allies' can provide for us, then our suspicion of them is likely to continue for a long time.

In making these comments, I'm not attacking either Rickell or Crowther personally, or even their instrumental approach to disability politics, but their understanding of the issues involved. They may well genuinely believe that their advice and approach serves the interests of disabled people best. However, when they base their strategies on either ignorance or misinterpretations of our history, they are hardly in a good position to best serve the interests of disabled people. And because of their structural positions within disabling corporatism, they lay themselves open to the accusation that they are 'selling disabled people down the river' or putting their own interests first.

Personalizing the political in academia

It is not only in the sphere of disability politics that this tension between the individual and the collective is rife, but also in the academic arena, leading to an instrumental approach to disability studies. I have spent most of my working life developing and promoting disability studies within academia, but I do not intend to provide a detailed analysis of the relationship between the individual and the collective in the light of the growth of disability studies, as I and colleagues have attempted to do this elsewhere (Barnes, Oliver and Barton, 2002, Chapter 13). Instead, I want to provide some personal reflections on the development of disability studies and some of the issues it faces in attempting to build an emancipatory knowledge base while straddling the tension between academic instrumentalism and collective empowerment.

As I have indicated elsewhere, in the development of disability studies disabled individuals, including myself, played a critical part. For me, as a new academic trying to build a career within academia, I was always aware of the creative tension between the need to provide a rigorous discipline but also take seriously the personal and collective experiences of disabled people through their writings. I'm not suggesting that disabled people were incapable of contributing academically but that at that time, within academia, experience was not regarded as a proper basis for teaching or research.

Hence, while I would not presume to speak for others involved, my own approach to the development of disability studies adopted a certain amount of what I can only call 'academic instrumentalism'. I make this point advisedly because there are 'purists' within the disabled people's movement who see any form of instrumentalism as betrayal. Personally, I believe we are all instrumentalists in one way or another and usually, therefore, what we often end up arguing about are choices and tactics rather than fundamental principles. In other words, one person's compromise is another's step too far. I certainly have made plenty of choices and compromises in my life, some of which I'm proud and others which I regret.

During the 1980s, I was planning to write a book that looked at disablement in society. I had been inspired by Vic Finkelstein's *Attitudes and Disabled People* (1980), and I was still thinking about some of the issues I had raised in my PhD. From there, a proposal to look at the production of disablement within capitalist society emerged and I was successful in obtaining both a contract and a grant to take the project forward. When I began to do the background research I was taken aback at how little relevant material there was to draw on and I bemoaned this fact at the beginning of the book when it was published (Oliver, 1990).

Little over a decade later, what I have called 'the big book of disability studies' was published (Albrecht, Seelman and Bury, 2000). In many ways this was a staggering achievement, containing thirty-four chapters, 850 pages of densely packed type and the work of fifty scholars, disabled and non-disabled alike, from across the world. When I began work on my book in the 1980s, I couldn't have imagined that so much work could have been produced in such a short time. The book serves as a symbol of the rapid growth in disability studies throughout the world and the quality of scholarship it has attracted.

There is a but, however. The book is very expensive, initially only available in hardback and very difficult to handle. In other words it is not as accessible, in the broad sense of that term, as perhaps it should be. Because I was involved in the project I received a complementary copy, but I have to confess that for many years it has remained unopened on my shelf because it is too heavy for me to pick up and if I tried

I'm scared I might drop it on my foot. I'm sure people with other impairments also find accessing this stored body of collective knowledge problematic. If disability studies has a key role in creating an inclusive world for disabled people, and I believe it does, then it's a shame that the big book is not as inclusive as it might be.

Elsewhere in this edition I have already discussed the rise of disability studies in the universities and the opportunities it has created. Another great achievement of this has been the creation of the Disability Archive at the Centre for Disability Studies at the University of Leeds by Colin Barnes and his colleagues. It contains the writings of disabled and non-disabled people alike, many of which would have been lost in the mists of time or only available to a small number of people in the know. Much of the material in the archive documents our experiences as disabled people and our reflections on our lives. Access, of course, remains an issue, but it is free and potential users only need a computer and Internet connection.

Disability studies has also benefited from the fact that, since 1986, the journal *Disability and Society* has been an important vehicle for promoting and disseminating its ideas. When Len Barton approached me with the idea of setting the journal up, we were both clear that its central concern should be the disabling society and that disabled people should be fully included in all the activities. The editorial board has always tried to manage the journal with these things in mind, but in recent years, with the increasing academization of disability studies and the declining influence of the disabled people's movement, this has not always been easy.

Symptomatic of this, perhaps, is the increasing irrelevance of many of the articles in *Disability and Society* to disabled people and their families. As someone who no longer has to read articles about disability as part of my professional responsibility, I find there are fewer articles that have any relevance or interest for me and I often feel that they are written as academic exercises to promote the author's career and, as a consequence, tend to exclude rather than include non-academics. I'm not taking an anti-intellectual stance in saying this because I have always insisted that understanding the disabling society will require rigorous academic analysis and a great deal of intellectual work. But if such work is going to be part of an emancipatory project it cannot just be accessible to academics.

Recently, for example, an article appeared on 'rhizomatic parents' (Goodley, 2007), about the experiences of parents of disabled children. Not only do I not know what a 'rhizome' is but I didn't understand anything else in the article except the direct quotes of the parents. I could quote pages of text here but one short quote will suffice:

> The rhizome assumes very diverse forms, such as when rats swarm over each other. The rhizome includes the best and the worst: potato, couchgrass or the weed. When typical conceptions of modernist discourse are flattened, the terrain is reconceived and ways of territorializing this terrain have to be reconsidered. Whilst we are all capable of occupying occasional positions of unity, popping out of the surface like the beginning of trees, we are also engaged in flux, clandestine movement and a multiplicity of growth. (Goodley, 2007, p. 150)

When I first attempted to read this paper I wondered for whom it had been written and whether the intellectual work involved in trying to understand it was worth it. In some ways it reminded me of the hoax Alan Sokal, a physics professor, played when he submitted an article that made no sense at all to a leading postmodernist journal. It was, however, accepted for publication in *Social Text*, despite the fact that Sokal (1996) littered his text with inaccuracies and jokes. A week after publication Sokal confessed that his paper was a hoax and his deception made headlines all round the world and beyond the academic press. The postmodernist response ranged from denial to denigration and even to betrayal; perhaps they were engaged in 'flux, clandestine movement and a multiplicity of growth'. As I've never met the 'rhizomatic parent' of a disabled child, I keep hoping Goodley's paper was another hoax, but I don't think it was.

One final reflection on the state of disability studies today is necessary herein. During the 1990s, disability was beginning to establish a foothold in academia and, as well as new courses coming on stream, I can think of at least ten single-authored books that contributed to the development of the subject. By the millennium, disability studies had established itself as a legitimate subject of enquiry and the following decade saw the creation of several new chairs, a variety of new courses and a Disability Studies Association. However, despite this growth, the number of single-authored texts that take the subject forward has declined almost to zero.

Tom Shakespeare (2006) did produce such a volume, but its advanced publicity promised much more than it actually delivered. It promised to break new ground by introducing 'critical realism' to the subject but instead it remained locked in the past. Predictably, the social model was castigated yet again and the medical profession and the big charities were endorsed and reinvented as the true allies of disabled people. In a review of the book, I concluded that, 'If that's the best that an emergent disability studies can do, I'm glad I've retired' (Oliver, 2007).

It is also true to say that while the disabled people's movement and disability studies had created a productive partnership in the 1980s and 1990s this no longer appears to be the case. No new ideas to sit alongside the big three generated in the 1980s have emerged or been developed within disability studies and it could be argued that too much time has been wasted on arguing about the existing ones, most notably in respect of the social model (Oliver, 2004). Further links between academia and the movement have not been nurtured in the way that they might (see Barnes, Oliver and Barton, 2002, Chapter 13). This is not solely because pressures on academics have forced them to adopt a more instrumental role, but also because the declining influence of the disabled people's movement has left them without much support in developing an emancipatory project within an inherently conservative academia.

In making these critical comments, I'm not seeking to minimize the difficulties faced by individuals attempting to build their careers while attempting to make a contribution to the emancipatory project that disability studies should be. Nor am I attacking individuals like Goodley and Shakespeare personally. A certain amount of instrumentalism is undoubtedly necessary in order to survive in the cut-throat world that academia now is, but I am concerned that the balance between personal advancement and collective empowerment has gone too far. While this has undoubtedly resulted in some superb individual scholarship, the knowledge generated does often remain inaccessible to most disabled people. It would be a shame if all the work that has gone into disability studies over the last thirty years were only to result in expanding the career opportunities of a few academic instrumentalists.

Politicizing the personal in the real world

So far, I have used the concept of instrumentalism to examine the relationship between the individual and collective in the disabling society. However, I'm not suggesting that our emancipatory project to create an inclusive one is merely a matter of making narrow choices about political tactics. The founding fathers of sociology taught us long ago that life was much more complicated than that. Robert Michels, a German sociologist who studied under Max Weber, produced a classic text on this very issue (Michels, 2001). He wanted to understand why many of the great socialist parties of the early twentieth century who were so opposed to what they called a 'war of capitalism' dramatically changed their minds when the First World War was declared. His conclusion was that all organizations became oligarchies and that, consequently, the leadership pursued its own interests rather than those of their membership.

In the previous edition of this book, I was hopeful that this fate would not befall the disabled people's movement, principally because I felt that our bedrock experiences of our impairments would prevent us from experiencing the same fate as many other social and political movements who have seen their leaderships build their individual careers on the basis of the collective experiences of their memberships without doing very much to improve these collective experiences. However, as we have seen in the decline of the disabled people's movement and the consequent rise of disabling corporatism, the oligarchical tendencies of these organizations have seen the leadership moving away from its bedrock experiences. This has been compounded by the blurring of the lines between disabled and non-disabled leaders of disabling corporatism.

Consequently, we have seen a disabling elite emerging in all three of the arenas I have discussed in this chapter. What's more, we cannot simply assume that these three arenas are all independent of each other because prominent individuals often inhabit all three. Indeed, I have occupied all three at various times in my life and, as I have already indicated, I'm not immune from the dangers I'm now discussing. But at least I recognize these dangers and have made myself unpopular in the past by talking about the guilt I feel about it both on public platforms and in my writings. There is a danger that as we become circulating elites moving between each arena, we move even further away from the everyday reality of the majority of disabled people. It then becomes easier to believe that because we have a nice life, everyone else does as well and, even if they don't, we are still fighting on their behalf rather than pursuing our personal careers.

While this fairy story allows us to go to sleep happy, I no longer believe it for two reasons. The first concerns our past history. I may be getting older but I remember life without the disabled people's movement when the big charities pursued their own limited agendas and government ignored us. The fact that that situation has changed is largely down to the collective struggles of disabled people to build a better life for ourselves and we have dragged reluctant charities and governments with us. That these two interests have now formed a disabling corporate alliance should now be a matter of grave concern because the question remains whether this circulating leadership elite will continue to pursue their own personal agendas while continuing to pay lip service to our collective ones.

The second reason why I don't believe the fairy story is because there is no evidence to support it in other arenas of political life. We only have to look at our circulating political elite to realize how easy it is to become divorced from the everyday reality of those interests they are supposed to serve. They move effortlessly between Parliament, industry, the professions and the statutory and voluntary sector, swapping one sinecure for another and often holding several at once. At the same time, they vote themselves ever larger pensions while cutting everyone else's; they use the Courts to render themselves immune from public scrutiny; and they continue to stick their noses in the trough of a political system that is at least 200 years out of date.

For these two reasons I cannot agree with the Shakespeares and Crowthers of this world who now appear to believe that disabling corporatism offers us the best chance of building a fully inclusive society. I'm not arguing against instrumentalism in the world as it is but we cannot build a better world for disabled people unless we can create a democratic movement in which our collective views can be advanced. We need a strong disabled people's movement to nurture and support those working in disabling corporatism and to hold them accountable for what they do and say.

My back pages

In my own struggles to understand disability there have been dark days as well as those of golden light. In my personally dark days one of the quotes that I have always held onto comes from the work of Carlos Castaneda (1998, p. 157) who once wrote, 'We either make ourselves miserable or make ourselves strong. The amount of work is the same.' I have found this valuable in my own personal struggles, but I believe it can also be applied to our political agenda. To paraphrase Castaneda, 'We can either build an exclusive society or an inclusive one. The amount of work is the same.' Crucial to this is developing an understanding of disability. For the second time, I have shared my struggles to do this with you and taken you with me on a journey through social theory, policy and practice, as well sharing many of my own personal experiences. I hope that I have helped in your struggles to do the same. However, I apologize, once again, if I have wasted your time.

Bibliography

Abberley, P. (1987) 'The Concept of Oppression and the Development of a Social Theory of Disability', *Disability, Handicap and Society*, vol. 2, no. 1, pp. 5–19.

Abercrombie, N., Hill, S. and Turner, B. (1988) *The Penguin Dictionary of Sociology* (London: Penguin).

Albrecht, G. (1992) *The Disability Business* (London: Sage).

Albrecht, G., Seelman, K. and Bury, M. (2000) *Handbook of Disability Studies* (London: Sage).

Althusser, L. (1971) *Lenin and Philosophy and Other Essays* (London: New Left Books).

Banyard, P. (1991) 'Research Director's Report', *ISRT Newsletter*, no. 23.

Barnes, C. (1990) *Cabbage Syndrome: The Social Construction of Dependency* (London: Falmer Press).

Barnes, C. (1991) *Disabled People in Britain and Discrimination* (London: Hurst & Co.).

Barnes, C. (1992) *Disabling Imagery and the Media: An Exploration of the Principles for Media Representation of Disabled People* (London: Ryburn Publishing and BCODP).

Barnes, C. and Mercer, G. (1996) *Exploring the Divide: Illness and Disability* (Leeds: Disability Press).

Barnes, C. and Mercer, G. (2004) (eds) *Implementing the Social Model of Disability: Theory and Research* (Leeds: Disability Press).

Barnes, C. and Mercer, G. (2006) *Independent Futures: Creating User-led Disability Services in a Disabling Society* (Bristol: Policy Press).

Barnes, C. and Oliver, M. (1995) 'Disability Rights: Rhetoric and Reality in the UK', *Disability and Society*, vol. 10, no. 1.

Barnes, C. and Oliver, M. (1998) *Disabled People and Social Policy: From Exclusion to Inclusion* (London: Longman).

Barnes, C. and Oliver, M. (2006) 'Disability Politics and the Disability Movement in Britain: Where Did It All Go Wrong?', *Coalition*, August, pp. 8–13.

Barnes, C., Oliver, M. and Barton, L. (eds) (2002) *Disability Studies Today* (Cambridge: Polity Press).

Bauman, Z. (1992) *Intimations of Postmodernity* (London: Routledge).

Bauman, Z. (1998) *Work, Consumerism and the New Poor* (Buckingham: Open University Press).

185

Beardshaw, V. (1988) *Last on the List: Community Services for People with Physical Disabilities* (London: King's Fund Institute).

Bickenbach, J., Chatterji, S., Badley, E. and Ustin, T. (1999) 'Models of Disablement, Universalism and the International Classification of Impairments, Disabilities and Handicaps', *Social Science and Medicine*, vol. 48, pp. 1173–87.

Brown, H. and Smith, H. (eds) (1992) *Normalization: A Reader for the Nineties* (London: Routledge).

Bury, M. (2000) 'A Comment on ICIDH2', *Disability and Society*, vol. 15, no. 7, pp. 1073–8.

Campbell, J. and Oliver, M. (1996) *Disability Politics: Understanding Our Past, Changing Our Future* (London: Routledge).

Castaneda, C. (1998) *The Wheel of Time* (Harmondsworth: Penguin).

Chappell, A. (1992) 'Towards a Sociological Critique of the Normalization Principle', *Disability, Handicap and Society*, vol. 7, no 1.

Clark, C., Dyson, A. and Millward, A. (1998) *Theorising Special Education* (London: Routledge).

Clough, P. and Barton, L. (eds) (1999) *Articulating with Difficulty: Research Voices in Inclusive Education* (London: Paul Chapman).

Cohen, S. (1985) *Visions of Social Control* (Oxford: Polity Press).

Coleridge, P. (1993) *Disability, Liberation and Development* (Oxford: Oxfam).

CORAD (1982) *Report by the Committee on Restrictions against Disabled People* (London: HMSO).

Corker, M. and French, S. (eds) (1998) *Disability Discourse* (Buckingham: University Press).

Craig, G. and Mayo, M. (1995) *Community Empowerment: A Reader in Participation and Development* (London: Zed Books).

Crow, L. (1992) 'Renewing the Social Model of Disability', *Coalition,* July.

Crowther, N. (2007) 'Nothing Without Us or Nothing About Us?', *Disability and Society*, vol. 22, no. 7, pp. 791–4.

Dalley, G. (1992) 'Social Welfare Ideologies and Normalization: Links and Conflicts', in H. Brown and H. Smith (eds), *Normalization: A Reader for the Nineties* (London: Routledge).

Davis, K. (1987) 'Pressed to Death', *Coalition News*, vol. 1, no. 4.

Davis, K. (1993) 'On the Movement', in J. Swain, V. Finkelstein, S. French and M. Oliver (1993), *Disabling Barriers – Enabling Environments* (London: Sage).

Denzin, N. (1997) *Interpretive Ethnography: Ethnographic Practices for the 21st Century* (London: Sage).

Despouy, L. (1991) *Human Rights and Disability* (New York: United Nations Economic and Social Council).

DHSS (1988) *A Wider Vision for the Blind* (London: Department of Health).

Disability and Society (1996) Special Issue, *Disability and Development, Disability and Society*, vol. 11, no. 4.

Disability Tribune Newsletter (1998) vol. 3, p. 2 (London: Disability Awareness in Action).

Driedger, D. (1988) *The Last Civil Rights Movement* (London: Hurst & Co.).

Driver, S. and Martell, L. (1999) 'New Labour: Culture and Economy', in L. Ray and A. Sayer (eds), *Culture and Economy After the Cultural Turn* (London: Sage).

ENIL (1989) Press Release 'European Network on Independent Living'.

Estes, C., Swan, J. and Gerard, L. (1982) 'Dominant and Competing Paradigms in Gerontology: Towards a Political Economy of Ageing', *Ageing and Society*, vol. 2, no. 2.

Fine, M. and Asch, A. (eds) (1988) *Women with Disabilities: Essays in Psychology, Culture and Politics* (Philadelphia: Temple University Press).

Finkelstein, V. (1980) *Attitudes and Disabled People: Issues for Discussion* (New York: World Rehabilitation Fund).

Finkelstein, V. (1988) 'Changes in Thinking About Disability', unpublished paper.

Finkelstein, V. (1993) 'Disability: A Social Challenge or an Administrative Responsibility', in J. Swain, V. Finkelstein, S. French and M. Oliver (1993), *Disabling Barriers – Enabling Environments* (London: Sage).

Finkelstein, V. (1994), personal communication.

Finkelstein, V. (1996a) *DAIL* (London: Disability Arts in London).

Finkelstein, V. (1996b) 'Modelling Disability' workshop at Breaking the Moulds Conference, Dunfermline, Scotland.

Finkelstein, V. (1996c) 'Outside "Inside Out"', *Coalition*, April, pp. 30–6.

Finkelstein, V. (1999) 'A Profession Allied to the Community: The Disabled People's Trade Union', in E. Stone (ed.), *Disability and Development: Learning from Action and Research on Disability in the Majority World* (Leeds: Disability Press).

Finkelstein, V. (2002) 'Whose History???', paper presented at Disability History Week, Birmingham.

Finkelstein, V. (2004) 'Phase 3: Conceptualising New Services', Conference: Disability Studies: Putting Theory Into Practice, Lancaster University, 26–8 July.

Finkelstein, V. and Stuart, O. (1996) 'Developing New Services', in G. Hales (ed.), *Beyond Disability: Towards an Enabling Society* (London: Sage).

Flynn, R. and Lemay, R. (eds) (1999) *A Quarter Century of Normalization and Social Role Valorization Evolution and Impact* (Ottawa: University of Ottawa Press).

Foucault, M. (1972) *The Archaeology of Knowledge* (New York: Pantheon).

Foucault, M. (1973) *The Birth of the Clinic* (London: Tavistock).

George, V. and Wilding, P. (1994) *Welfare and Ideology* (Hemel Hempstead: Prentice Hall).

Giddens, A. (1990) *The Contradictions of Modernity* (Cambridge: Polity Press).

Giddens, A. (1994) *Beyond Left and Right: The Future of Radical Politics* (Cambridge: Polity Press).

Giddens, A. (1998) *The Third Way: The Renewal of Social Democracy* (Cambridge: Polity Press).

Gillespie-Sells, K. (1993) 'Sing if You're Happy that Way', *Rights Not Charity,* vol. 1, no. 2.

Gillespie-Sells, K. and Campbell, J. (1991) *Disability Equality Training: Trainers Guide* (London: CCETSW).

Gillinson, S., Huber, J. and Miller, P. (2006) *Disablist Britain: Barriers to Independent Living for Disabled People in 2006,* SCOPE with DEMOS and Disability Awareness in Action.

GLAD (2000) 'Reclaiming the Social Model of Disability', Greater London Action on Disability conference, February.

Goodley, D. (2007) 'Becoming Rhizomatic Parents: Deleuze, Guattari and Disabled Babies', *Disability and Society,* vol. 22, no. 7, pp. 145–60.

Gough, I. (1979) *The Political Economy of the Welfare State* (Basingstoke: Macmillan).

Gouldner, A. (1975) *For Sociology: Renewal and Critique in Sociology Today* (Harmondsworth: Pelican).

Green, D. (1993) *Reinventing Civil Society* (London: Institute of Economic Affairs).

Hammersley, M. (2000) *Partisanship and Bias in Social Research* (Buckingham: Open University Press).

Harrison, P. (1992) *The Third Revolution* (London: I.B. Tauris).

Hasler, F. (1993) 'Developments in the Disabled People's Movement', in J. Swain, V. Finkelstein, S. French and M. Oliver (1993), *Disabling Barriers – Enabling Environments* (London: Sage).

Hearn, K. (1991) 'Disabled Lesbians and Gays Are Here to Stay', in T. Kaufman and P. Lincoln (eds), *High Risk Lives: Lesbian and Gay Politics After the Clause* (Bridport: Prism Press).

Hellander, E. (1993) *Prejudice and Dignity: An Introduction to Community Based Rehabilitation* (Geneva: World Health Organization).

Hellander, E., Mendis, P., Nelson, G. and Goerdt, A. (1989) *Training the Disabled in the Community* (Geneva: World Health Organization).

Hevey, D. (1992) *The Creatures Time Forgot: Photography and Disability Imagery* (London: Routledge).

Higgins, P. (1985) *The Rehabilitation Detectives: Doing Human Service Work* (London: Sage).

Hill, M. (1994) 'Getting Things Right', *Community Care Inside,* 31 March.

Hills, J. (1995) *The Future of Welfare: A Guide to the Debate* (York: Joseph Rowntree Foundation).

HMSO (1998) *New Ambitions for Our Country: A New Contract for Welfare* (London: HMSO).

Holdsworth, A. (1993) 'Our Allies Within', *Coalition,* July.

Humphreys, S. and Gordon, P. (1992) *Out of Sight: The Experience of Disability 1900–1950* (Plymouth: Northcote House).

Hurst, R. (2000) 'To Revise or Not To Revise', *Disability and Society*, vol. 15, no. 7, pp. 1083–8.

Independent Commission on Population and Quality of Life (1996) *Caring for the Future: Making the Next Decades Provide a Life Worth Living* (Oxford: Oxford University Press).

Jameson, F. (1991) *Postmodernism, or the Cultural Logic of Late Capitalism* (London: Verso).

Jordan, B. (1998) *The New Politics of Welfare* (London: Sage).

Keith, Lois (ed.) (1994) *Mustn't Grumble* (London: The Women's Press).

Kerzner Lipsky, D. and Gartner, A. (1997) *Inclusion and School Reform: Transforming America's Classrooms* (Baltimore: Paul H. Brookes).

Kuhn, T. (1970) *The Structure of Scientific Revolutions*, 2nd edn (Chicago: University of Chicago Press).

Lee, P. (2002) 'Shooting for the Moon: Politics and Disability at the Beginning of the Twenty-First Century', in C. Barnes, M. Oliver and L. Barton (eds), *Disability Studies Today* (Cambridge: Polity Press).

Leonard, P. (1997) *Post-modern Welfare: Reconstructing an Emancipatory Project* (London: Sage).

Lukes, S. (1974a) *Individualism* (Oxford: Basil Blackwell).

Lukes, S. (1974b) *Power: A Radical View* (London: Macmillan).

Mannheim, K. (1936) *Ideology and Utopia* (London: Routledge and Kegan Paul).

Martin, J. and White, A. (1988) *The Financial Circumstances of Disabled Adults* (London: HMSO).

Martin, J., Meltzer, H. and Elliot, D. (1988) *OPCS Surveys of Disability in Great Britain: Report 1 – The Prevalence of Disability among Adults* (London: HMSO).

Martin, J., White, A. and Meltzer, H. (1989) *Disabled Adults: Services, Transport and Employment* (London: OPCS).

Marx, K. (1913) *A Contribution to the Critique of Political Economy* (Chicago: Chicago University Press).

Michels, R. (2001) *Political Parties: A Sociological Study of the Oligarchical Tendencies of Modern Democracy* (Ontario: Batoche Books).

Mongon, D. (1982) *Special Education and Social Control* (London: Routledge).

Morris, J. (1991) *Pride against Prejudice* (London: Women's Press).

Morris, J. (1992a) *Disabled Lives* (London: BBC Educational).

Morris, J. (1992b) 'Personal and Political: A Feminist Perspective in Researching Physical Disability', *Disability, Handicap and Society*, vol. 7, no. 2.

Morris, J. (1992c) 'Tyrannies of Perfection', *New Internationalist*, no. 293, July.

Nirje, B. (1993) *The Normalization Principle – 25 Years Later* (Helsinki: Institute for Educational Research).

Oakley, A. (2000) *Experiments in Knowing* (Cambridge: Polity Press).

O'Connor, J. (1973) *The Fiscal Crisis of the State* (New York: St Martins Press).

Oliver, M. (1978) 'Medicine and Disability: Steps in the Wrong Direction', *International Journal of Medical Engineering and Technology*, vol. 2, no. 3.

Oliver, M. (1979) 'Epilepsy, Self and Society', PhD thesis, University of Kent.

Oliver, M. (1980) 'Epilepsy, Crime and Delinquency: A Sociological Account', *Sociology*, vol. 14, no. 3.

Oliver, M. (1982) 'My Disability was the Best Thing That Ever Happened to Me', *Guardian*, 24 February 1982.

Oliver, M. (1983) *Social Work with Disabled People* (Basingstoke: Macmillan).

Oliver, M. (1989) 'Conductive Education: If it Wasn't so Sad it Would be Funny', *Disability, Handicap and Society*, vol. 4, no. 1, pp. 197–200.

Oliver, M. (1990) *The Politics of Disablement* (Basingstoke: Macmillan and St Martin's Press).

Oliver, M. (1992) 'Changing the Social Relations of Research Production', *Disability, Handicap and Society*, vol. 7, no. 2, pp. 101–14.

Oliver, M. (1995) 'Does Special Education have a Role to Play in the Twenty-First Century?', *REACH: The Journal of Special Needs Education in Ireland*, vol. 8, no. 2, pp. 67–76.

Oliver, M. (1996a) 'Defining Impairment and Disability, Issues at Stake', in C. Barnes and G. Mercer, *Exploring the Divide: Illness and Disability* (Leeds: Leeds University Press).

Oliver, M. (1996b) *Understanding Disability: From Theory To Practice* (Basingstoke: Macmillan).

Oliver, M. (1997) 'Emancipatory Research: Realistic Goal or Impossible Dream?', in C. Barnes and G. Mercer (eds), *Doing Disability Research* (Leeds: Disability Press).

Oliver, M. (2001) (with Delamont, S. and Connolly, P.) 'Essays on Partisanship and Bias', *British Journal of Sociology of Education*, no. 1, pp. 157–68.

Oliver, M. (2003) 'Selling Out: Should We Care?', *Coalition*, November, pp. 20–3.

Oliver, M. (2004) 'If I Had a Hammer: The Social Model in Action', in J. Swain, S. French, C. Barnes and C. Thomas (eds), *Disabling Barriers: Enabling Environments*, 2nd edn (London: Sage).

Oliver, M. (2007) 'Disability Rights and Wrongs: A Review' *Disability and Society*, vol. 22, no. 2, pp. 230–4.

Oliver, M. and Bailey, P. (2002) *Report on the Application of the Social Model of Disability to the Services provided by Birmingham City Council* (Birmingham: Birmingham City Council).

Oliver, M. and Barnes, C. (1997) 'All We are Saying is Give Disabled Researchers a Chance', *Disability and Society*, vol. 12, no. 5, pp. 221–40.

Oliver, M. and Barnes, C. (2008) '"Talking About Us Without Us?" A Response to Neil Crowther', *Disability and Society*, vol. 23, no. 4, pp. 397–9.

Oliver, M. and Hasler, F. (1987) 'The Role of a Self-help Group in Overcoming Disability: A Case Study of the Spinal Injuries Association', in A.O. Frank and G.P. Maguire, *The Management of Disabling Diseases* (London: Heinemann Medical Books).

Oliver, M. and Sapey, B. (1999) *Social Work with Disabled People. 2nd Edition* (Basingstoke: Palgrave).

Oliver, M. and Sapey, B. (2006) *Social Work with Disabled People. 3rd Edition* (Basingstoke: Palgrave).

Oliver, M. and Zarb, G. (1992) *Personal Assistance Schemes: An Evaluation* (London: Greenwich Association of Disabled People).

Oliver, M., Zarb, G., Silver, J., Moore, M. and Salisbury, V. (1988) *Walking into Darkness: The Experience of Spinal Injury* (Basingstoke: Macmillan).

Papadakis, E. (1993) 'Interventions in New Social Movements', in M. Hammersley (ed.), *Social Research: Philosophy, Politics and Practice* (London: Sage).

Pfeiffer, D. (2000) 'The Devils are in the Details: The ICIDH2 and the Disability Movement', *Disability and Society*, vol. 15, no. 7, pp. 1078–82.

PMSU (2005) *Improving the Life Changes of Disabled People: Final Report* (London: Cabinet Office).

Rabinow, P. (ed.) (1984) *The Foucault Reader* (New York: Pantheon).

Richardson, J. (1999) *Common, Delinquent and Special: The Institutional Shape of Special Education* (London and New York: Falmer Press).

Rieser, R. and Mason, M. (1990) *Disability Equality in the Classroom: A Human Rights Issue* (London: ILEA).

Rosenblum, K. and Travis, T. (2003) *The Meaning of Difference*, 3rd edn (New York: McGraw Hill).

Rothman, D. (1971) *The Discovery of the Asylum* (Boston: Little Brown).

Royal College of Physicians (1986) *Physical Disability in 1986 and Beyond* (London: Royal College of Physicians).

Ryan, J. and Thomas, F. (1980) *The Politics of Mental Handicap* (Harmondsworth: Penguin).

Scull, A. (1977) *De-carceration. Community Treatment and the Deviant: – A Radical View* (New York: Prentice Hall).

Shakespeare, T. (1993) 'Disabled People's Self-organisation: A New Social Movement?', *Disability, Handicap and Society*, vol. 8, no. 3, pp. 249–64.

Shakespeare, T. (2006) *Disability Rights and Wrongs* (London: Routledge).

Shakespeare, T., Gillespie-Sells, K. and Davies, D. (1996) *The Sexual Politics of Disability* (London: Cassell).

Silverman, D. (1998) 'Research and Social Policy', in C. Seale (ed.), *Researching Society and Culture* (London: Sage).

Slee, R. (1998) 'The Politics of Theorising Special Education', in C. Clark, A. Dyson and A. Millward, *Theorising Special Education* (London: Routledge).

Sokal, A. (1996) 'Transgressing the Boundaries: Toward a Transformative Hermeneutics of Quantum Gravity', *Social Text*, nos. 46/7.

Stuart, O. (1992) 'Race and Disability: What Type of Double Disadvantage', *Disability, Handicap and Society*, vol. 7, no. 2.

Sutherland, A. (1981) *Disabled We Stand* (London: Souvenir Press).

Swain, J., Finkelstein, V., French, S. and Oliver, M. (1993) *Disabling Barriers – Enabling Environments* (London: Sage).

Taylor, D. (1996) *Critical Social Policy: A Reader* (London: Sage).

Thomas, C. (1999) *Female Forms: Experiencing and Understanding Disability* (Buckingham: Open University Press).

Tomlinson, S. (1981) *A Sociology of Special Education* (London: Routledge and Kegan Paul).

Turner, B. (1984) *The Body and Society* (Oxford: Basil Blackwell).

UPIAS (1976) *Fundamental Principles of Disability* (London: Union of the Physically Impaired Against Segregation).

Walton, J. (1979) 'Urban Political Economy', *Comparative Urban Research*.

Warnock Report (1978) *Report of the Committee of Enquiry into the Education of Handicapped Children and Young People* (London: HMSO).

Wendell, S. (1996) *The Rejected Body: Feminist and Philosophical Reflections on Disability* (London: Routledge).

Wilde, O. (1966) *Complete Works* (London: Collins).

Williams, F. (1989) *Social Policy: A Critical Introduction* (Cambridge: Polity Press).

Wolfensberger, W. (1989) 'Human Service Policies: The Rhetoric Versus the Reality', in L. Barton (ed.), *Disability and Dependency* (London: Falmer Press).

Wolfensberger, W. (1994) 'A Contribution to the History of Normalization with Primary Emphasis on the Establishment of Normalization in North America between ca. 1967–75', in R. Flynn and R. Lemay (eds) (1999), *A Quarter Century of Normalization and Social Role Valorization Evolution and Impact* (Ottawa: University of Ottawa Press).

Wood, P. (1980) *International Classification of Impairments, Disabilities and Handicaps* (Geneva: World Health Organization).

Wood, R. (1996) quoted in *Disability Now*, April.

Young, J. (1999) *The Exclusive Society* (London: Sage).

Zarb, G. and Nadash, P. (1994) *Cashing in on Independence: Comparing the Costs and Benefits of Cash and Services* (Derby: BCODP).

Zarb, G. and Oliver, M. (1993) *Ageing with a Disability: What Do They Expect After All These Years?* (London: University of Greenwich).

Index